HOW TO BUILD A CHILD'S CHARACTER

BY TAPPING INTO YOUR OWN

Dr. Stephen Birchak

Royal Fireworks Press
Unionville, New York

Royal Fireworks Press
First Ave, PO Box 399
Unionville, NY 10988
845 726 4444
FAX: 845 726 3824
email: mail@rfwp.com
website: rfwp.com

ISBN: 978-0-89824-665-0

Printed in the United States of America on acid-free paper using soy-based inks by the Royal Fireworks Printing Company of Unionville, New York.

TABLE OF CONTENTS

ACKNOWLEDGMENTS

George Bernard Shaw once said, "Life is a flame that is always burning itself out, but it catches fire again every time a child is born." Every time a person taps into their character, a flame catches fire again and in order for this book to be completed, it also required a lot of small fires. I would like to acknowledge the following people for their support and inspiration in the creation of this book.

All of the children, parents, and professionals whose stories and examples are contained in this book are the important flames. All their accounts have been altered in order to protect their privacy. While some portraits are composites, and others have biographical details that have changed, it is their heart, spirit, and energy that has guided me and kept my flame alive.

Dr. Tom Kemnitz, of Royal Fireworks Press, for his patience, understanding, and his belief in the importance of character in our children.

The College of Saint Rose for its support, vision, and commitment to the development of children.

My wonderful friends and colleagues, who kept encouraging me to see this book through.

Sean, Perry, Pam, Donna, and Nicole for their kind words of support.

My family, for putting up with me. My sons, Brandon and Nick for their love, laughter, and character. My wife Annie, for her unconditional love, direction, and a flame that never flickered. She is, without a doubt, the most sincere, genuine, and authentic model of character that I have ever known.

Creating a frame of mind for the five lessons

> **Pretty much all of the honest truth-telling there is in the world is done by children.**
>
> **Oliver Wendell Holmes**

Some of my favorite time during the week is when I am in schools working with children. I help to create and implement Character Education programs with teachers and counselors, and I treasure the interactions that I have with children during those times.

Children are the most genuine human beings on earth. There's no other energy in the world quite like that of a child's. They wear their emotions and thoughts on their sleeves, and they soak up the world like a dry sponge.

Not long ago I sat with a group of fifth-grade boys as we were going through a lesson on bullying, being picked on, and being left out. Their energy was in high gear. They were honest, interested, and excited about the activity. In my group I had nine boys, and each one of them seemed to have a story or a thought on the subject.

When I was young, I had the nickname "Birdie," and years ago it somehow turned into "Dr. Bird." Since it's easier for most kids to remember, I continue to go by "Dr. Bird." On this day, the students were calling out my name and really getting involved in the lesson. The hands were in the air and the stories were flowing, "Oh, Dr. Bird, I remember...oh, Dr. Bird, there was this kid..."

As a group counselor, one of my favorite things to do is to watch body language while I listen to the words being said. On this day, the boys had bodies that screamed! When we talked about bullies or being included in the "popular" groups, you could see some arms folding, while others sat on their hands. Some boys leaned in, and others leaned out. A couple of boys stared off in deep thought while others nodded. By looking around the group, you could tell who was popular, unpopular, dominant, passive, shy, or boisterous. They were a pretty fair representation of children we find in every group, every school, and in every neighborhood.

On this occasion I was telling the boys about my own youth to see if they could relate to being "different." Right now as an adult, I am only four feet, nine inches tall, so you can imagine how short I was when I was in school (one of my colleagues once told me that the reason why I connect with kids is because I see eye-to-eye with most of them). I was telling the boys that since I was always the shortest one in my class, I was usually the last to be picked for many of the gym class games.

There was one boy in my group by the name of Aaron. He was also the shortest in this group of fifth graders, and every day we had our group, he would sprint to the chair that sat directly to my left. You wouldn't have to be a genius to figure out that he identified with my short stature.

As we talked about the issues and how it felt to be a part of the "in group" or the "out group," the children offered their stories and viewpoints. Even the known bullies in the group were beginning to connect with the feelings of others. I kept waiting for little Aaron to say something, but he didn't. He watched,

2

listened, held his hand to his chin, nodded, squinted, and remained in deep thought. The discussion continued, and soon we were at the end of the lesson and listening to everyone's final thoughts. Again, Aaron sat in silence. I asked the boys for their last thoughts, and I did a final visual scan looking from side to side in the group until my eyes connected with Aaron's. "Any other comments?" I asked. I desperately hoped that he would add his two cents worth.

Aaron paused, looked up at me, and nodded. He then reached up and patted my shoulder as he spoke, "You know something Dr. Bird?" His look became more serious.

"What's that Aaron?"

"Even though you were picked last, and sometimes left out, you know what I think?"

"What's that Aaron?"

"Dr. Bird, I think you turned out okay."

I'm not ashamed to admit that I was touched. The scene has stuck with me for two very important reasons; first, children are a lot more sensitive than we give them credit for. We don't have to tell them what to feel or how to feel. They are in tune with their world, and they are sensitive to the little things that make or break their lives. Second, all children desperately want to form a connection with something or someone who can understand what their life and future is all about.

What was most amazing about Aaron was that he was probably the one who suffered the most from school cliques and bullying, yet in the discussion, his mind went to thoughts about me, and he wondered how I felt. I know adults who own only a fraction of the empathy that Aaron had. I appreciated his vote of confidence. I think that he has very good chances of turning out

3

okay. As he looked at me that day, he must have figured *if this short guy did okay, then I can too, I've got good chances too.*

For those of us who have been a part of a child's life as a teacher, parent, counselor, or one of numerous other guiding roles, I think that we all hope that he or she turns out okay. In other words we want him or her to have a productive and peaceful life. "Turning out okay" can mean a lot of things; it can be accomplishments, success, and independence. For the most part though, we simply want children to enjoy life. We want them to laugh, celebrate the wonders of this beautiful world, and most of all we want them to feel loved.

When I grew up in southwest Denver, I spent a couple of my high school summers going to an evening wrestling program at a neighboring high school. It was about a ten-minute drive from where I lived. Years later, when I was living in New York, I remember turning on the television and seeing that school again. Students were running out of the doors that I used to walk through everyday. They were running in a state of fear and panic. Single file with their hands over their heads, they tried to make their way to safety. Students inside their school were murdering other students. It was Columbine, a school where I spent a lot of time, a school where I competed, and a school that I knew well. Like most others who watched, it was enough to make me cry. It was a sad loss of life and potential. Since that time, we've seen even greater acts of aggression. Most of us never imagined the acts of hatred that we are experiencing today.

The question before us is this—what would keep a young man like Aaron from bringing a gun to school? What would keep him from becoming angry or despondent? What could we do for him so that he could laugh, love, and live life the way it should be? What lies in the gap between the child who turns out okay, and the child who goes on a murdering spree?

4

The answer is in the each of us. *We,* the adults, are the link to a child's future. *We* are the ones responsible for determining whether the child will have a healthy connection to the world or an unhealthy one. A child with character has developed a toolbox of skills to deal with life's expected and unexpected challenges. Aaron is on the outer fringe of popularity, and he will have to deal with all of the issues that come with that status. Many children will have it much rougher than Aaron, and many will have it much easier. It's not the challenges that will make or break these children, it's their life-skills that will help them to succeed, and these skills are more possible if they have a healthy connection to healthy adults.

What will a child like Aaron have in his toolbox to deal with life's challenges? He will have what we adults give him—piece by piece.

In the past few years, I have made presentations and conducted workshops for thousands of teachers, counselors, parents, and other groups who work with children. I believe that all of these wonderful people are trying their hardest to find appropriate tools for children. I admire people who work with children because I believe that the most important jobs on this earth are those that involve our youth, whether they are in or out of the home.

After every workshop there are always a number of people who approach for questions or comments. Some ask for other resources, and others have specific questions that require complex answers such as, "What do you do when a child won't take any personal responsibility?" We could spend days examining our culture, the world, influences, family, and morality. I would love to have the perfect prescription, "Try two character education exercises and call me in the morning!" Oh how I wish it were that easy!

The solution is not in a ten-minute recipe but in life-skills that are continually developed over the course of a lifetime. No one learns how to deal with life "once and for all." Most of us know from our own experiences that we have a lot to learn about ourselves, and we hope to keep on learning for as long as we live.

The world is filled with beautiful new experiences that are just waiting to be discovered, just like Aaron's smile, and they are around every corner. The world can also be a frightening place. Statistics alone are enough to shock any of us. The World Health Organization estimates that on an average day, 1,424 people are killed in acts of homicide. Suicides outnumber the homicides. The statistics are not the problem; they only describe a changing world. They are the symptoms of human beings who have lost respect for others' lives and in many cases have given up on the sacredness of their own lives as well.

In the sixties we had "duck and cover." Now we have crisis response teams, metal detectors, school lock-downs, and full time police officers in the building. Educators and administrators not only have to learn curriculum, they are also being trained to deal with bomb threats, violent parents, lawsuits, and hostage situations. One teacher told me she was having nightmares because of the Professional Development day at her school. Teachers once looked forward to Professional Development days when they could be involved in some workshop where they learned a new way to teach. This junior high school teacher reported that at her school they brought in a team of police officers who would hold rubber guns on them and teach them how to deal with hostage situations. It's no wonder she's having nightmares!

These are only the situations *in* the schools! We pick up the paper every day and see reflections of death, terror, violence, domestic aggression, and road rage, and these are in our neighborhoods! At times it seems overwhelming, and it feels like we are up against an insurmountable battle.

The bottom line however is this: **it is a problem that can be solved**. We must not allow our fears to cause us to give up. If

6

we created it, we can solve it, but it's important to develop an understanding of what *will* change the problem and what won't. In other words, we need to spend less time obsessed with the problem, and more time consumed with the solution. We hear ourselves saying, "If only the government…the laws…the schools…television…the internet…Hollywood…would do *this*…then the problem would be taken care of." All of these things we wish would be different only represent the symptoms of individuals changing. We have no right to complain about any of these issues if we are weaving in and out of traffic, screaming at a waitress, backhanding our children, verbally abusing the clerk at the checkout line, or throwing out sarcastic barbs at a co-worker with whom we don't get along. These are the behaviors that are changing the world, and if we want our children to grow up with strong life-skills, then we have to begin with every teachable moment that comes our way. Our contributions to the status of the world have to do with our own day-to-day and minute-to-minute exchanges with others.

We have to make up our minds about how we will respond to the hostilities in the world and about whether or not we will decide to join them. When our heads hit the pillow at night, we need to reflect on whether we did more giving or taking today. If we call ourselves "caring" people, then we have to walk the talk. We can't beat kindness into people, and if aggression is our only tool for responding to aggression, then we are part of the problem.

The world is a wonderful place filled with extraordinary opportunities to make a difference, and the biggest battles do not reside outside of us—they are within our own hearts. If we want change, we have to make the change.

We have to have commitments that match our desires. It's like anything else in life; it's the action that matters, not the wish. For example, I'm the king of the roller coaster diets, and

7

I'll gain ten pounds then lose five, then I'll gain ten and then lose fifteen, and on and on. The proof is only found in what can be measured—the results. The proof is in the doing, not the saying. If my body were the product of my *desires,* I would look like Charles Atlas himself for 365 days out of the year. I'm loaded with desires. Unfortunately, my body is the product of my *commitments*, and there is a huge difference between the two. If I'm not committed to my combat strategies in the war with ice cream, my body will show the carnage. Having only the *desire* to win a war will never be enough. It's one thing to speak of character and kindness; it's another to live it.

I would be the last person to say that I could live a perfect life with no emotional bruising. All of us are less than perfect. The difference has to be found in day-to-day small commitments to become a reflection of the kind of world that we really want for our children.

The Quest for the "Magic Wand"

Any person who has invested in the life of a child can easily come to the same conclusion: there is no magic wand. There is no perfect recipe for guiding a child toward a full life. The world will always be less than perfect, thus our goal must be for progress not perfection.

While it is true that there is no perfect recipe, it is also true that adults and children have the remarkable strength to adapt and overcome a great number of trials in their lifetimes. All of us can think of well-adjusted people who have grown up with an environment, parents, or trials that would seem to have pointed them toward disaster, yet despite these circumstances, they became strong adults. In most cases, there was a significant adult whose strong influence guided them toward a full life.

Adults who have strong character can always point to a figure in their lives. They will say, "I had a mother...father

8

> **If the world were perfect, it wouldn't be.**
>
> **Yogi Berra**

...teacher...coach who..." Our goal is to be that person. We need not be perfect, but we must try to grow more each day.

What is equally amazing is that there is no set age for turning a life around. We hear people say, "when I was seven I was influenced by a great teacher... when I was twelve, my mother helped me... when I was sixteen, I had this coach who believed in me... when I was in my thirties and my life was going down hill, I had this boss who gave me a chance..." There is no particular time in our lives when we cease to have the capacity to change and to grow; it can happen at any time. We all know people who have changed, and they all shared one commonality—they welcomed change. As the old saying goes—If we keep doing what we are doing, we will keep getting what we are getting.

I've spent a lifetime admiring and studying the power, resilience, and beauty of the human spirit. Humans have made tremendous strides in science, knowledge, and technology. It's time we also made even greater strides in human compassion. We need to decide whose shoulders we want to stand on. There have been tyrants, tormenters, oppressors, dictators, and bullies who have filled the pages of our history books. There have also been people like Gandhi, Martin Luther King, and Mother Theresa who have altered human history. In our day-to-day lives, we need to think about which path we will choose, even if it's only done with small acts.

We need to face the reality about our future and the possible options for paths of harmony or hostility for our children. The place to start is in two fundamental truths. **First, our children are not born broken.** They all come with carbonation. There are a lot of people who would rather not believe it. We hear it in such things as, "he's just a bad kid." Children are growing, developing human creatures. They are people who are in the process of becoming something. They, like ourselves as adults, are unfinished products who have the potential to become "broke," or the potential to have effective life-skills. The overwhelming majority of all human beings have the potential for lives filled with hope, compassion, and goodness. Which leads to our second truth—what is the main driving force for becoming broke? Or becoming fixed?

Children are the carbonation of life.

Dale Howard

Secondly, and importantly, we, the adults, are the ones who are responsible for shaping the growing child. There is no classroom, curricula, or program that by itself saves a child, and in most cases the child alone doesn't have the personal resources to take control of his or her life and make the right choices. We can have the world's greatest character education program or the very best curriculum, but it is worthless if it lacks human compassion. One of the myths we've created about raising children is the belief that information will save them. If this were true, then we would be living in a moral paradise because they have more information than any other generation. The problem is using wisely all the information we have. Children today are learning about pipe bombs, oral sex, and drugs every day over the internet. Who knows what they will be learning five years from now? What they need is a person. What they need is time in strong relationships with caring adults who can guide them through a complicated world. If we, as caregivers for children cannot embrace this single rudimentary concept, we are useless to guide them.

This book offers no step-by-step recipe; it does however offer some basic human truths. I can give a family suggestions like planning family meals, increasing quality time, and communication skills, but prescriptive recipes are not the answer. The answer is in developing the *character* that will allow us to create all of our recipes. Our goal is to build our character so that we can make good decisions, and to build a child's character so he or she can make good decisions.

Even if I could give someone an exact plan to follow for a child who *lies* about "who broke Mom's vase?" we would need to create a whole new one for "how to stop hitting your brother," and another for "keeping my kids off drugs." This book lays the foundation for understanding what character looks like. It's not about recipes and gimmicks; it's about facing ourselves, and living our lives with character. The gimmicks come, and the gimmicks go. To offer you a set of recipe gimmicks does nothing to create a lifestyle. To offer you the ability to examine the formula for character will allow you to look at the bigger picture of our lifestyles.

The formula for character in children is the same for adults. The five most important lessons that will shape a child are the very lessons that each of us as adults need to review **every** day of our lives. Our foundation is in our lifestyle.

First, we have to insist on *Civility*. Civility is characterized by respect for others, and it begins by developing self-respect. If we compromise civility in our own behavior, we compromise our integrity. Civility has nothing to do with *what* we are communicating, or agreeing, or disagreeing about. It has to do with

11

the process of *how* we are communicating—with respect and self-dignity. We know that children who exercise greater civility are more highly respected, have more personal control, and are more likely to develop personable communication skills.

Secondly, a strong *Conscience* must be developed for a guiding life philosophy. A strong conscience is a combination of empathy and ethical behavior. In our era of instant personal gratification, it's become more common to disregard the needs of others and thus risk the harmony of our personal relationships. Children who have developed a strong sense of conscience have fewer incidences of trouble with authority and the law, and fewer lifelong incidences of violence. They also have a greater likelihood of developing successful skills in leadership, as well as making greater contributions to society.

Third, the skills of *Resilience* must be taught and developed throughout our lives. Resilience is not only characterized by the ability to overcome life's obstacles, but most importantly it also includes the ability to enjoy life fully in spite of these trials. It's one thing to survive, it's another thing to survive and maintain optimism and joy. Children who possess the skills of resilience have a greater sense of self-worth and are higher achievers in school. Resilient people in general tend to have fewer lifelong mental and physical health problems, as well as greater longevity.

Fourth, *Collaboration* is an essential skill for a harmonious and full life. It is the backbone of human progress. Collaboration is something entirely different from obedience, yielding to others, or controlling others. It is the ability to honor each other's needs, seek each other's opinions, and free others of the bonds of oppressive domination. Children who develop strong collaborative relationships are less likely to be motivated by control or abuse. Children who learn strong collaborative and communication skills also tend to have longer and more gratifying relationships during the course of their lives. They also tend to have less stress connected with their family and relational struggles.

> # You must become the change you wish to see in the world.
>
> ## Gandhi

Fifth, human *Kinship* is the key to unlocking the door to a fruitful social future. Children who learn acceptance and understanding of our human differences at an early age have a greater ability to deal with change and are less likely to develop racism or sexism during the course of their lives. Children who learn the bigger picture of social justice tend to become more tolerant as well as becoming advocates for other children who are bullied and abused. They also have greater chances of becoming lifelong learners as well as supporters of democracy and human rights.

As human beings, we all come with faults and flaws. Even the best among us are less than civil, less than caring, and less than fully cooperative on our bad days. In spite of all our faults, *we* are the best source of everything a child needs. We must work as hard as possible not to be perfect, but to keep that source strong and thoughtful. We will determine the future. We need to try to become the person we want them to be.

Many of us grew up in households that we remember for the bad things—the tempers, alcohol, impatience, anger, insults, and aggression. We may even remember how we slowly disconnected and then spent a lifetime trying to reconnect. If given the option, wouldn't we want to give our children something better than we had? For all the animosity that exists in the world, do we really want to become a memory that they resent?

13

A common myth that many of us believe is that we are doomed to repeat the patterns of our past. This is simply not true. We are only doomed to repeat the past if we make conscious decisions to keep acting in a manner that we know to be less effective. It's not written in stone that we have to become abusers, alcoholics, or violent even if we came from these homes.

We're in the process of making small moments of someone's personal history, even if it's just a child's memory of a classroom, or a family dinner, or a learning moment. It's wonderful to think of all the power we have to shape a child's life. Using that power responsibly is the most important task we will ever have.

Practicing Civility sets the Ground Rules for Integrity and Respect

"Oh, Dr. Bird! Come here please, I have to show you something!"

Every week when I finished my character education program with this second grade class, a young boy, Josh, would herd me over to his desk where we had a weekly ritual of going through his folder of keepsakes. The folder grew fatter as the year progressed, and it contained every special piece of paper in this boy's life. He had awards, glittery pictures, paintings, colorings, A+ spelling tests, and A+ math tests. He was proud of his folder, and the glow on his face told the whole story.

On this day we went through all of the items, and it occurred to me that the folder was like a sacred vault in his desk. I said, "Josh these are so beautiful, why don't you ever take any of these home?"

At the moment that I asked the question, Josh immediately changed. His smile turned to a frown, he quickly gathered his items, stuffed them in the folder, and sat in silence with his arms folded at his desk. I then asked Mrs. Trudell, the teacher, "What was that all about?"

She went on to tell me how Josh's mother would take any item or event that was special in his life and threaten him with it. If he had an A+ spelling test that he shared with her, she would use it to discipline him by screaming and tearing it up in front of him when she was mad at him or upset that he didn't "behave." If they had a "special" day at school or "field day" or "going to the firehouse," Josh would not show up, because

15

again if it were special in his life, she would use it to punish him.

Josh was identified with multiple emotional disorders including anxiety, impulse, and behavioral dysfunctions. I believe that most of these were because of the series of psychological tortures that his mother put him through. One day he came to school with tears running down his cheeks. When Mrs. Trudell asked him what was wrong he said, "My mother said she was going to come to school today and tear down my "Student of the Week" award. He pointed to the award that the teacher mounted on the wall just one week ago.

Josh's tears dried up when Mrs. Trudell assured him, "No one, and I mean no one will ever take awards off the wall in our classroom. I guarantee you that it will hang there until the end of the school year."

The sad reality about children like Josh is that there are thousands of them who endure these types of abuse every day. They come from homes where they never feel connected to any adult, and they never have a single day when they feel special. Later in the year Josh came to school in tears again. It was his birthday. He reported that his mother told him he was, "too much of a bad boy to get any present this year."

Fortunately for Josh, he had a wonderful birthday. It was only because he had a guardian angel who also happened to be his teacher. Every time I visited Mrs. Trudell's class, someone was feeling special. While we see a world of children who are devastated by their environment, it's important that we also keep our eyes open to see those people who are affecting children in miraculous ways.

The difference is in exercising civil rather than abusive behaviors. Some people among us think about every behavior they are engaged in with the intent of bringing kindness to others.

Others are steamrollers with little knowledge or thought about the destruction they are causing.

Mrs. Trudell's class is loaded with children who are identified with emotional and behavioral problems. It's a self-contained special education classroom. I've seen children in her room begin to fall apart late in the day, or late in the week, or just before a school vacation. In most cases the child doesn't even know why, but it's because they are leaving the safest and warmest place they know. You ought to see these kids when they get off the school bus. They know they won't be hurt all day because they are with Mrs. Trudell. This is one of the best places on earth for them, and they are excited to be there.

I've seen what masterful teachers and parents do with their children, and it all comes down to a kind, selfless person—it's civil behavior all day long. Civility combined with thoughtfulness can make any of us feel special.

In Mrs. Trudell's classroom, each child gets a week when he or she is crowned "Special Student." For Mrs. Trudell's students, it's also a weekly writing assignment (she's one of those teachers who ties issues of self-esteem and "character" into all of her lessons). The assignment is to write a paragraph about the things you like about the special student. Sometimes they are just little things, but the students eat them up like candy. "He has a nice smile...can run the fastest...is a good colorer...can spit farther than anyone..."

The unique thing about Mrs. Trudell's class is that each student gets his or her week, no matter what, and for some students, it's easy to tell that this is the only place that they get to feel that they are something special. She has a whole ceremony, after a day of privileges, and pampering. She bestows a "Special Student" certificate after reading all of the other students' paragraphs. One certificate goes on the wall, and one is given to the child.

Many philosophers have written about such questions as, "Do I exist? What is the meaning of my life?" Many of us will never be as lucky to have moments like these in our lives. I've seen children in her classroom melt, turn red, scream with glee, and writhe in ecstasy as they are being recognized as a "Special Student." There is no existential dilemma taking place in this child's life at that moment. Life is not only meaningful, it is wonderful!

The shame is that little boys like Josh have to hide their certificates in a folder because they are afraid to show Mom what a wonderful thing they have. It's also a shame that research shows us that children like Josh have a much greater chance for serious mental illnesses during the course of their lives. He has one environment that is warm and loving, and another that is cold and abusive.

Mrs. Trudell also did similar things with her own family. Everyone is entitled to a night off from chores once in a while, and on that day the family also does rounds at the dinner table and says, "One thing I like about my sister Katie is…"

In order to build civility, we have to recognize that incivility is becoming a social norm where a "good fight" is held in higher regard than a mutual solution. Just like in the case of Josh, his mom won the fight, but destroyed the relationship. Any trust, respect, or love that she could hope for is gone.

We have to think about the little things that are extensions of our frustrations. If we are not consciously trying to build an environment with civility, then we are apt to think of only our own needs. The mother who abuses Josh isn't aware that she is dramatically increasing his chances for becoming a violent teenager—he will be the next generation of abusers. Every time a snappy comeback or control of others is more highly valued than a kind word, it's taking its toll on humanity. This chapter will look at civility from a number of angles to help us recognize it, create it in our own children, and promote it in our everyday life.

To stop incivility in its tracks, it takes work and self-examination. First, we need to look at **the "Wolves" who are raising our children**, and how the environmental scenery is changing for our youth. We will also look at **three immediate changes that anyone can make to improve the civility** in our lives and how we can **measure our personal changes**.

Civility comes from a lifestyle that is geared toward respect. At the core of the lesson of civility is the issue of "respect," in which we need to **promote self-respect**, and public respect. The chapter will look at what works and what doesn't work.

Tying things together, the chapter will emphasize **our role as an agent of change**, and give insight as to what we can and cannot control.

By teaching civility we set the foundation for character. A child or an adult with civility has the ability to create a positive effect on others. Civility also allows for greater personal growth because the individual can interact and communicate with emotions and thoughts intact.

Learn to Recognize the Wolves But Don't Join Them

Remember those stories about a child being lost in the woods and being raised by wolves? The child was abandoned, and he had to develop survival skills. In time he began to think and act like a wolf. He used every ounce of human ingenuity to adapt to his surroundings and have his needs met. Then, when placed back with humans, he was wildly out of control because he only knew what he had learned.

Many of today's children have been abandoned as well. They haven't been abandoned to a cave or the woods; in fact they inhabit every neighborhood, every city, and every school. Some have a lot of money, some don't. Some are geniuses; others have average intelligence. They come in all sizes, nationalities, religions, and backgrounds.

When our children are abandoned, they are left to the mercy of the wolves, and today's youth are spending most of their waking hours with the wolves. We know from research that the average American child will spend 5-6 minutes of face-to-face quality time with his or her parents in the course of a day. One in four children says she or he has *no* adult figure to confide in. This isn't news to parents; in one recent survey more than half of today's parents believe that their own parents did a better job than they are doing now. Only a third of today's parents believe they are doing a good job of teaching values.

When we think of the story of the child being raised by the wolves, we obviously can't blame the child. He is living what he is learning. Our modern day's wolf den is much more subtle, and the influences are covert.[*] Some of these wolves are on television, the internet, video games, gangs, cults, and unfortunately some are the parents of the child, just like Josh's. The child is not at fault.

Children are brilliant creatures who learn survival skills in whatever environment they are raised. They learn to adapt, improvise, and overcome whatever they see as obstacles in their lives. If we want to remove them from the wolf den, then we need to put a lot more time in the family den.

Children's minds (just like adults' minds) are constantly trying to solve problems by using the information that is available to them. It's not just the hardcore influences either; it's the little things they hear everyday. For example, in a recent scene from the number one, prime time sitcom, one of the main characters walks into the coffee shop, points to her friend and says, "You had sex today didn't you! I can tell by the look on your face."

The scene was humorous to most adults, but what does the average twelve year-old do with that information? I can't imagine how I would have reacted at that age, and what conclusions I would have drawn about healthy relationships if Mr. Brady from the "Brady Bunch" walked into the kitchen and said to the housekeeper, "Alice, you had sex today didn't you! I can tell by the look on your face!"

These kinds of subtle influences may seem innocuous, but the results are shocking. In a recent documentary, the lives of average middle-school girls in an upper-middle-class suburban school was followed for a week. They talked about providing oral sex for their twelve-and thirteen-year-old boyfriends like it was just a walk in the park.

In addition to many children lacking respect for themselves, they are growing up in a culture where anti-authority is placed on the highest pedestal. In today's culture, authority is the enemy rather than the benevolent protector. I recently had lunch with one of my former high school teachers. He said that once he looked forward to Mondays. The students were respectful, and he said he often said to himself, "I can't believe they pay me to do this." Toward the end of his career however, the incivilities grew, the belligerent parents were in droves, and the disrespect was overwhelming. He described the way students once presented themselves, respected themselves, and demonstrated a sense of reverence for the wisdom of authority figures. "It wasn't that they disagreed with us any less than kids do today, it was *how* they disagreed that made it easy, and they didn't spit in your face and threaten to sue you. The reason they were respectful to authority was because if they were rude they would be letting themselves down." His message was clear—self-respect creates public respect.

Disagreeing with authority is certainly everyone's right, but to have blatant disregard for authority is counterproductive. The

21

number one criterion of an Anti-social Personality Disorder is a disregard for authority, and some sociologists contend that we may be raising a generation of anti-socials. Why would anyone want to be a coach, teacher, administrator, or a cop in today's society? You instantly become a member of the enemy! Forget the fact that you joined the profession for any noble reason of helping people—you are now the enemy.

Even though the status regarding respect in our culture is a little depressing, the great news is that we can make some small changes that can begin to effect civility in our daily lives.

One-Minute Reflection: The Wolves

Each night for one week, examine what was stressful about the day.

1.   Write down from one to five interactions with others (adults or children) that were the most stressful.

2.   Now place a check next to those where your reaction was to "join the wolves." Include any of the following:
_____raised your voice
_____humiliated someone
_____used sarcasm
_____insulted
_____called someone a name
_____gave someone the passive-aggressive "quiet treatment"
_____used a tone of voice that was hurtful.

3.   Next to each interaction write "can repair" or "can't repair" for the relationship. If you can repair the relationship (and you have to decide whether it's worth it or not), name one thing you could do differently. Make a decision about each relationship, and underline those things you *will* do differently.

Turning the Tide **Today**: Three Quick Steps to Changing the Path of Incivility

The worst thing we can do about incivility is to complain about it. The best thing we can do is alter its course. We can't get civility with more aggression, so we have to choose other methods of relating to others—especially children! We need a plan, and it starts with three basic changes that can be utilized instantly. We have to pay attention to the process of our communication, place more value on our relationships than our personal needs, and maintain an assumption of good will in others.

Our patience will achieve more than our force.

Edmund Burke

Step One:
Pay more attention to the *process* of our communication than the *content*.

Think about the last time you were involved in a disagreement that became emotional, abusive, or aggressive. Chances are it had less to do with *what* you were talking about, and it had more to do with the *manner* in which people addressed one another. It's okay to be passionate about an issue; it's another to insult, attack, or become abusive when trying to make a point.

When your fifteen year-old comes in the door and presents an "attitude," or a "tone of voice," or a "sarcastic remark," about doing the dishes, it's important that we address *how* we are communicating so we can find a common ground of mutual respect in order to address intelligently how we don't see eye to eye.

If either one of us has a tone of disrespect, we can expect one more connection between us to be severed. It is most important to realize that our own incivilities may be producing these behaviors.

When we use incivilities, what do we expect in return? When we sarcastically scream, "Well, well, well I can see that my energetic kids have once again cleaned the kitchen like I asked them!"

We must be expecting them to think—*I'm glad Mom yelled at us like that. I feel so much closer to her now, I see the error of my ways, and it's easy for me to know exactly what she wants. Perhaps I shall run to her, hug her, and thank her for this new wisdom she has imparted to us!*

Using incivilities and insults are a waste of breath. Just like our children, when we are attacked like this, we are ready to fight back, either with a snide remark, a few slammed cabinets of our own, or more sarcasm. It would take just as much time to give them a direct message that would not allow for the battle of disrespect by saying, "Kids, I need you here in front of me right now." Then, looking into their eyes and saying, "I need your help. We've talked about trying to work as a team to keep this house clean, and I am disappointed that jobs were not done like I asked you to do."

By using this kind of direct communication, we didn't beat around the bush, insult, attack, or demean—we got to the point. It's okay to express our disappointment, and to remain as the authoritative figure, but being in authority doesn't give us the right to overstep the boundaries of mutual respect.

In order for children (or anyone for that matter) to feel indebted to us, we need their respect. We also need to set the format for communication and *not* hand out fodder for a battle. The same holds true for us on our jobs, when your boss insults you with a tone of voice, or disrespects you, how do you respond? *I'm so glad he was abusive to me. Those insensitive remarks give me that warm feeling inside that make me want to be around him more and work harder for him!*

If it doesn't work for us, it won't work for children either. In order to build mutual cooperation, we need mutual respect. We may get snapped at, we may get lashed at, but if we respond with more aggression, we are not creating the kind of process we need. It is our right in *any* conversation with *anyone* (child or adult) to stop the process and say, "I deserve the right to be treated with respect. Let's start over...."

If we compare it to dog or horse trainers, the last thing we ever hear them say is, "You know, if you beat an animal enough, it will always come back for more love..." Any animal trainer will tell you that if you abuse the animal and back it into a corner, it will come back looking for an opportunity to trample you because it's just trying to survive. You can beat down a four year-old verbally, but watch out when he or she becomes sixteen years old and is big enough to fight back..

How can we expect others to respond to us with civility if *our* process of communication is abusive? Those who are quick to step over the line of abuse in communication don't possess appropriate boundaries to begin with. They can't give what they don't have—they can't offer respect without self-respect.

Step Two:
Place more importance on the relationship than on your personal need.

This doesn't mean that your need is not important. In fact, your need may be of vital importance, but placing more value on the relationship does two things—it preserves your mutual respect, and it respects the integrity of others. Just because I

25

have an important need, I don't have the right to stomp all over everyone in the process.

If we examine the qualities of calm and peaceful people, we will notice that they approach every interaction by focusing on the relationship before the task. On occasion, if we are confronted with an emergency, we may have to bark for help and not consider the relationship, but those times are rare (although there are some people who believe that they have about fifty emergencies a day). There are times when it would be ineffective to say, "Hey Judy, you have a sad look on your face, is your day going okay? I really hate to interrupt you in the middle of your coffee, but if it wouldn't be too much trouble, could you gently place your foot on the brake before the car rolls over me and crushes me to death dear?" We don't always need niceties in times of crisis, but if we are having more than about one crisis a week, we need to realize that the only real crises are taking place in our heads. (For the record, please note a few of the following things that are not a crisis—long lines, stuck in traffic, crying babies, socks on the floor, caps off the toothpaste, late for school, poor restaurant service, and spilled milk.)

Peaceful people approach their children, spouses, co-workers, bosses, custodians, secretaries, and friends all in the same manner. Peaceful people are genuine, they are sincere, and they bring warmth to the exchange. They start interactions with, "Good morning! Nice to see you, how is your day?" They have a genuine interest in the relationship because the relationship is what's most important to them. They know that if our relationships are strong and intact, then the jobs will get done with much greater efficiency.

On the other hand, we also know the stompers who are interested in finding out whether you can meet *their* needs first, "I need this done by... I want you to... You need to... Is your homework done? Did you get the dishes done? Did you...?"

We quickly learn that they simply aren't interested in *us;* it is *I* they are interested in first. You can hear it not only in their words but also in their tone and voice inflection. They maintain intimidation because it's easier for them to produce than a relationship. It's hurtful, and often it's insensitive, but most of the time it's just plain selfish.

> **In every verbal exchange we have during the course of a day, we have the option of giving a gift of kind words or bruising someone with harsh words.**

Civility begins and ends with others' needs being at least as important as one's own. It feeds off of one of the oldest lessons that we have heard since we were children. The old *"do unto others,"* is a timeless concept that begins with seeing others as human beings and not *objects to meet my personal needs in this world.* The strongest character is a patient character.

People who exercise civility also have a foundation of impulse control. If others' needs are viewed as important as our own, we will not see every inconvenience as a threat. When we stop seeing life as a threat and stop losing our tempers, we become more genuine. Our habits change into lifelong patterns. We see people's faces, and we don't just turn on civility to manipulate others—we live civility because it's an extension of ourselves. We realize that it's not just something that we turn on for special people or a special situation—the waiter in the restaurant deserves as much kindness and respect as your best friend.

Step Three
Live with an assumption of good will

People with strong characters will trust that most human beings are good by nature. It's okay to be cautious in this world, but some take it to paranoia, and they rarely assume good will in others. It's as though they believe the whole world is inherently bad, and *you'll have to prove to me otherwise!*

It's easy to fall into this trap because the hostile people in this world own the headlines, and every time we believe that they represent the status of all human beings, they are winning the war. Civility assumes that people are basically good in nature, and our habitual reaction is not one of defensiveness, suspicion, or paranoia, or mistrust. We are born with this **assumption of good will**, and it may be one of the most important things to cling to when it seems like everyone else is giving up.

In my neighborhood there was a boy named Donnie. He was a pleasant seven-year-old with a contagious smile and an effervescent spirit. One day he was walking door-to-door with his grandmother selling candy bars for a school fundraiser (it's a shame we have to raise funds for school this way). He knocked on a few doors before getting to his first response. From the sidewalk the grandmother could hear a couple of words that included "...not interested!" before she witnessed the slamming of the door. Donnie ran back to the sidewalk and breathlessly asked his grandma, "Grandma! Can you lend me a dollar?"

"Why do you need a dollar?" she asked.

Donnie replied, "Grandma, she was in a really bad mood and said she didn't have any money for candy. I want to buy her a candy bar because I know that she would feel better if she had one!"

The grandmother was bothered by the reaction of the person behind the door, but followed her instinct, gave him a dollar, and let him go back to the door.

She then noticed the woman at the door talking to him as he extended his arm in the gesture to give her the candy bar. She then disappeared and returned for a few more words of exchange.

After Donnie ran back to his grandma, she waited for his story, unsure of what to expect. "I told her I wanted to buy her the candy bar," he said. "You know, so she could feel better, then she said maybe she didn't look hard enough for her purse the first time. Then she found it and bought **two** candy bars. Isn't that great grandma!"

The story is a wonderful illustration of a person who hasn't lost his *assumption of good will* in his fellow human. He believed the grumpy woman when she said she didn't have money, but was not affected by it because he didn't interpret her actions as anything but truthful. He followed his own good nature and actually changed the woman who was rude to him. It's amazing how so much wisdom can be learned from a seven-year-old who hasn't given up on his faith in his fellow human beings.

The pessimist will say, "Just give him enough time! He will learn what people are really like!" Unfortunately he may take a few of those isolated incidents and lose his trust in others, but we should hope he doesn't. We hope he doesn't grow into one of those pessimistic grumps we often meet.

Some would contend that we need to be mistrustful to protect ourselves because "they are always out to get you!" We have to be cautious and aware of life's dangers, but if we spend our lives in mistrust, we become blameful and jaded. There are a lot of peaceful people who are able to maintain their assumptions of good will and still be astutely aware of scams and shady people when they meet them. We have to remember that if we lose our assumptions of good will in others, it will be replaced by paranoia and mistrust.

Effective leaders in general are *not* naturally distrustful—they have maintained and nurtured their assumptions of good will on others' behalf. You notice it because they foster trust and mutual respect in their relationships. If you want to measure the effectiveness of leadership in a parent, teacher, or boss, notice how workers, or children, or students act in their absence. If the children are out of control, then it tells you that they are motivated by fear, not by the mutual goals of the relationship.

I've seen offices where the workers' behaviors are dramatically altered depending on whether the boss is there or not. On the day that the boss leaves, it's like a scene from the *Wizard of Oz*—the secretaries are dancing in the aisles singing "Ding Dong the Witch is dead! The Wicked Witch is dead!" This tells you that they are motivated by fear, not a sense of duty to the team. The same holds true for the children who get into trouble every time they are left to supervise themselves, whether at home, at a playground, or at school. In the parents' presence they are motivated by fear of Dad or Mom's reaction, not a personal sense of debt to themselves or the family's values.

One-Minute Reflection: Good Will

What was my first reaction the last time I felt mistreated? Did I immediately label someone as a "jerk," "brat" or "idiot" who got on my nerves? What about on my job? In my family? In public?

1. List one to five people who contributed to a miserable part of your day and write your reaction to each.
2. For each person you labeled, create a re-frame for him or her, for example: STUPID IMPATIENT JERK!!—to: He must have just been in a hurry or
   THAT MAN HAS NO HEART! HE IS A MAJOR KNUCKLE HEAD!—to: How sad for him to be so self-consumed.
   THAT BRAT IS OUT OF CONTROL!—to: He's got some very ineffective survival techniques, what can I do to teach him more effective ones?
3. Now, look at your list and place a check mark next to those whom you feel it is impossible to assume good will for, should you cross their paths tomorrow. For each, ask yourself, What would keep me from re-framing his or her behaviors?
4. For each instance where anger or resentment was harbored, ask: Do I simply want to wallow in my anger toward him or her? How much personal power am I losing in the process? Does he or she deserve to have power over my life?

Measuring the Evidence of Our True Beliefs

> **Knowing is not enough; we must do.**
> **Willing is not enough; we must apply.**
>
> **Goethe**

Civility is measured by one's acts, *not* thoughts or beliefs. What we do and our verbal exchanges are representations of what we believe. There are decades of studies insisting that what is modeled to us has a great likelihood of becoming our own behavior. We can't believe for a moment that a child will become a considerate adult at a restaurant when all he or she has heard for years is a parent screaming, "Where the hell's my coffee! These biscuits are cold! You idiot! You fool! You brainless wonder! What the hell's your problem?"

In addition to modeling, we also need to understand that we have the power to stop incivilities by *not* reacting with aggression of our own. If we are in fact the smart, intelligent, and mature factor in this relationship, then we need to be the one who stops the chain of aggression cold in its tracks. This doesn't mean that we should be someone's doormat. It means that we need to become effective communicators, neither aggressive *nor* passive.

When we walk into a teacher's lounge on any given day, we can hear intelligent adults saying, "That Johnny knows where my goats are tied; that Johnny knows how to push my buttons; that Johnny knows how to get on my nerves." The teacher is personalizing the child's survival techniques and believing himself or herself a victim.

Every time we react to Johnny's behavior with our own curtness, or short-tempered responses—we continue the chain of aggression. If we really believe that we have a duty to change a child's behavior, we need to start with our own. It's like the parent who says to his or her child, "Don't hit your brother," then proceeds to backhand the child. What we do is powerful evidence of who we are.

Many of us can remember those people in our lives who showed tremendous kindness—even when we were being idiots (all of us have our moments). For me, I remember the second grade. When I was in the second grade, I was a bundle of fun. At least I thought I was. To the teachers, however I was hell on wheels. I was a class clown, full of energy, always in trouble, and I had my own chair in the principal's office to prove it. Today I would be labeled as "attention deficit," or "a misfit," or "emotionally disturbed."

Looking back on it now, I feel sorry for my teacher, Miss Burns. She tried everything under the sun, and nothing seemed to work. I was punished, I had detention, and on a regular basis I was in the principal's office. Miss Burns had run out of ideas and decided that she would invite a friend of hers into our classroom. His name was Mr. Sands, and he was this huge musclebound man with a GI crew-cut who taught fifth grade up on the second floor. On the day he visited our classroom, I was acting out in my usual manner. This time I was covering my desk with paste (we all remember that thick paste that came from those huge plastic jars and was rumored to be the product of horses melted down). Much to the delight of my classmates, they were soon overcome with giggles as they watched my antics. From the back of the classroom, Mr. Sands stood up and walked over to me. "Stevie," his barreling voice broke the air, causing the giggles to subside. "Stevie, I want you to come with me."

At that point I was actually scared for the first time in my career as an elementary school class clown. He took my hand and walked me down the hallway into an empty teachers' lounge. He picked me up, and stood me on a table to look at him straight in the eye. I tried to hold a bold grin, but inside I was shaking like a leaf. I certainly wasn't afraid of Miss Burns, and of course I had no fear of the principal, but this guy had me quivering in my little tennis shoes. He placed his two big hands on my shoulders and said, "Stevie, I think the world of Miss Burns. She is a very nice person, and she is trying to do her job the best she can, but every day she seems to have problems with a little boy named Stevie. Do you know what I mean?" My little head nodded. "Stevie, I really need your help because I want the two of us to come up with a plan to help Miss Burns. Do you think you might be able to give me a hand?" I was shocked at what I was hearing because I thought his plan was to crush me on the spot with those huge hands thus eliminating the nuisance in Miss Burn's class. He wasn't crushing me at all; in fact he was asking me for help and seeking my opinion.

He had a piece of paper, and we outlined all of the things that Miss Burns needed in order to do her job. Most of the suggestions came from me. I actually felt honored to be asked for an opinion. This was the first guy on earth who seemed to be interested in what I thought. To make a long story short, we had a plan in ten minutes that included how I could sit on my hands when I felt like throwing something, or put my hand over my mouth when I felt like blurting out an answer, and other simple ideas. In the end it was his patience, understanding, and his compliments on how he believed that little Stevie actually had the potential to become a leader.

"The other kids like you Stevie, but you are wasting all this good personality on dumb things. As you know Stevie, we only have three months left in school, and I have the task of identifying some of Schmidt Elementary's most helpful students. Each of us teachers have to identify a couple of student leaders to come back to school for a couple of days following the school year and help us to tear down our classrooms and shut down the school for the summer. You know what I think Stevie?" By this time my eyes were bulging as one word kept bouncing around in my little brain—"leader?" Who? Me?

I had no idea what he was thinking, so I listened intently, "Stevie, I think you could be on my list to be one of those special students who could help in my classroom. There are no rewards in this world for disruptive children, but there are plenty of rewards for students who help the school get its job done."

Wow! I was never put in a place like this in my life. He told me there would be no guarantees, but he was going to be working with Miss Burns to see if—little by little we could pull off this plan.

It was *very* difficult at first, but I kept thinking about what he said—*Me? A leader?* I did make little changes day by day, and I had to record them on my wide-lined Big Chief tablet. I slapped my hand over my mouth when I felt like clowning, I completely reduced my principal's office trips, and in the end I was actually feeling valuable in the classroom. He checked on me regularly, went over my tablet, and told me how proud he was of my progress—and this was coming from *the* Mr. Sands.

During the last week of school he told me that I earned a spot as one of the chosen students who would help him after the school year. You can't imagine the pride I felt to walk into that vacant school after the year ended and help him out. He even bought me a soda from the teachers' lounge when we had a break. It was the sweetest soda I ever drank.

Eventually I ended up in his fifth grade class where he was a master of combining firmness with fun. He taught with all the energy and liveliness that most teachers only dream of. We laughed, worked, and learned on a daily basis. After that year, I decided that one day I would be a teacher.

There are at least a dozen lessons in how he approached me that included patience, respect, empowerment, and nurturing. As a result, he changed my life. We all know that changing children is not always that easy, and that not all of our attempts end up with fairy tale endings, but for Stevie, his class clown energy was converted for life (although some of my grad students still accuse me of being a class clown).

One small side note to this story—a year after I left the school, Miss Burns married Mr. Sands. I shouldn't flatter myself, but I'd like to think that I was partially responsible for getting them together.

Mr. Sands was one teacher who really did make a difference in children's lives. Many of us have recollections of those people in our own lives.

Promote Self-Respect

We cannot give away what we do not possess. As mentioned earlier, if we have no self-respect, we cannot give respect. We need to promote self-respect by demonstrating what it is like to enjoy this body and this life that we occupy. Self-respect is different from ego-centric, selfish narcissism.

When we are two years old, we have only one goal, and that is to be king or queen of the universe. Unfortunately, there are many adults who have never outgrown their two-year-old rage and insist that they are still king or queen of the universe. This is the weakest manifestation of self-respect.

People with healthy self-respect deeply appreciate the role they have in this world and derive their pleasure from influencing others through positive behaviors. They value their own personal qualities that are productive and fruitful in the growth of others, and they try to eliminate their own personal behaviors that are destructive and insensitive.

> **Until you make peace with who you are, you'll never be content with what you have.**
>
> **Doris Mortman**

Self-respect also means self-love. Many of us know people who hate themselves. They live lonely lives, wishing others would love them, which is a ridiculous expectation. It's impossible for others to love them. Imagine self-hater Ralph introducing himself. "I would like you to meet Ralph, and I want you to love Ralph, I want you to appreciate Ralph and want you to be friends with Ralph. Personally, I can't stand Ralph—but it's important that you love him."

While Ralph's words may seem ridiculous—it's what people without self-respect do to others all the time! They say "I want you to love me—but I can't stand me!" They are asking others to do something for them that they cannot do for themselves.

Whenever you hear a thirteen year old scream, "I don't give a damn what anyone thinks of me," we have to remember that he is not lying. He really doesn't give a damn. There is no one in his life to give a damn to.

Think about adults you knew in your youth who constantly screamed for others to respect them. "You will respect me!" But, if they were jerks, the kids secretly laughed at them. It's like the tyrannical boss who insists on respect but never gives it. When they leave the office, the workers cackle just as the kids did. You can beat fear into people but not respect. The more that a child has adult figures treating him or her with respect, the more he or she will respect themselves. This will naturally cause civility and manners to emerge. It's more difficult for a self-respecting child to be belligerent. An act of rudeness becomes a loss of a sense of self, a feeling of being "bad" and an act of letting oneself's standards down.

Building a healthy self-respect works the same way in children as it does in adults. If we are labeled, insulted, and belittled on an ongoing basis, we begin to believe our lesser worth. I once had a thirty-seven year old mother of two children as a client in a counseling session. She described how her sense of self-esteem and self-worth had become distorted over a period of time. She said, "It took me years to understand what self-love really is. When I was growing up, the adults in my life had a habit of labeling 'me' instead of 'what I did.'"

She told me about her miserable life that was made up of adults who could only tell her what a bad person she was when she made mistakes. Instead of saying, "that was a mistake you made," they would say "there you go again—you idiot! Fool! Brat! Dumb! Lazy! Useless!"

As a result, throughout her adult life she could never give herself a break, and she couldn't keep from labeling herself every time she made a mistake. She was conditioned into negative self-statements every time something went wrong. Her competence and confidence took a downward spiral for years regardless of how intelligent or accomplished she became.

Her greatest fear was that her daughters would grow up with the same self-labeling lack of confidence. In therapy, she realized not only how she could change her daughters' futures but also how she could change her own as well. One day in a counseling session she practically bounced around my office in bundle of energy as she shared her revelation, "Do you know what has occurred to me? That I've never loved myself, and it has little to do with my mistakes. I seemed to be conditioned to giving myself negative self-talk as though I believed it was supposed to motivate me—in some distorted way. I didn't make any more mistakes than the average person, it's just that every time I did I hated myself! The mistake became the 'bad person,' and after a while I believed it."

She went on to describe her vow never to label her children as an "idiot, brat, or bad person." She said, "My girls are good girls who may make a lot of mistakes, but mistakes don't make them bad people. As an adult, the single biggest change in my life has been to realize that I may do some dumb things, but I am a good person. With self-realization, my whole world changed. I am kinder to myself for all of my faults." She went on to describe how much joy she was experiencing in seeing her daughters love themselves more than she did when she was growing up.

The woman's story is all too typical. We know that human beings will begin to believe what they hear, if they hear it enough. She didn't want the trend to continue.

All of us know people who can't love others because they can't appreciate their own lives. The most cruel, rude, and obnoxious people we meet in a day's time are mostly angry with themselves. The angriest children we know are the ones who hate their lives.

One-Minute Reflection: Mistakes

Name your five biggest mistakes this week. (The ones simply where you made an error in a decision or judgment.)

1. Next to each, indicate if you used a self-statement, such as "I'm late again, I am such an idiot..."
   "I forgot to put the money in my wallet, I am so stupid..."
   "That assignment didn't turn out the way I wanted, I am such a loser..."

2. Think about each instance of "personal labeling" that you did in the past week. How much of your energy did you forfeit in the process?

3. Now look at each to see if you could have reframed it from "person blaming" to "behavior changing," such as
   "I am late again; it was not smart to leave late; I'm going to need to create a new habit of early morning organization..."
   "I forgot to put the money in my wallet. I need to start paying attention to the details before I leave the house."
   "That assignment did not turn out right. I need to get some help and feedback to do it differently next time."

4. If you worked with children in the last week, if you used a label for them, reprise the entire experience. Did you see them as "brats... lazy... etc.?"

Promote Public Respect

> **It is not fair to ask of others what you are not willing to do yourself.**
>
> **Eleanor Roosevelt**

As we engage in behaviors that shape children, we must continually ask ourselves—would this work on me? It sounds simple, and it makes sense, but there are a lot of common practices in parenting and teaching that violate common sense. Let's imagine treating teachers the way we often see teachers treat students. For instance, if a faculty member at a school meeting was whispering, how should the principal deal with it? (Most of us know that faculty are notorious for whispering and passing notes during meetings.) Would we learn from public humiliation? *"Alright teachers, if you'll make a note, I'm writing Mr. Jones' name on the board and placing a checkmark after his name. Let's all pay attention to Mr. Jones in the back row of the meeting. Instead of whispering to Mrs. Phillips, why don't you share it with the rest of us?"*

Perhaps if that doesn't work, we should use the popular "sarcastic insult" (at a faculty meeting)—*"Well, well, well Ms. Smith, it looks like we are on time again, aren't we? Another productive day Ms. Smith? I would have never known."* Or perhaps we could try—*"Oh, so we need to borrow a pencil don't we Mr. Sullivan? I can see we are well prepared today as usual aren't we Mr. Sullivan!"*

Another overused ever-popular technique is to wait until a lot of people are around and exercise those vocal chords by voice raising—*"MR. ROBINSON, GET OVER HERE NOW!! YOU*

*ARE ON BUS DUTY AND I WANT YOU IN THE FRONT OF
THIS BUILDING NOW!! STOP, STOP, STOP RIGHT NOW
AND GET OVER HERE!"*

If we were treated on the job in the manner in which we often
treat our children and students, we would complain to our unions,
file a grievance, or seek another line of work. Why? Because
we've been violated, and we have rights! Perhaps we have to
grow old and grumpy before we actually inherit these rights.

How often have we seen parents berate their children in public?
Imagine if we had the same treatment. What if you asked the
waiter in a restaurant, *"Excuse me sir, where can I find the
restroom?"* How would we, as adults would feel if the waiter
suddenly started yelling at us, *"You should have known better
and gone at home! You are just going to have to sit there and
suffer. You'll go when I'm good and ready to take you there!
I don't care if you do have an accident, you should have thought
of that at home!"* It's as if people believe that simply because
they are parents they have a license to violate their children's
rights.

Aggression comes in a lot of forms. Publicly humiliation, sarcasm and screaming are some of the most inappropriate ways to
treat any human being. We should never believe that we have a
license to violate children with these acts of violence. We have
to imagine ourselves in their shoes. We need gentleness and
kindness, and so do they. Without it, they can only learn the
habits that we despise.

False pride and the need to "win" also destroys our connections
to others. One of the biggest errors we make in our relationships
is that we have the need to "win." "Winning" a confrontation
solves nothing because its only goal is to inflict pain and exercise
power. To humiliate someone publicly means that one never had
the goal of peace. When we raise our voices, it's usually more

42

of a statement about controlling someone than building an alliance or improving the relationship.

One-Minute Reflection: Winning?

How many disagreements did I need to "win" with others (adults and children) today?

1. If I had to re-examine the exchange, what possible scenarios could have occurred where we both could have won more understanding and more respect?
2. List the conflicts you had today. Next to each mark whether you gave them more kindness than they deserved, or exactly what you believe they deserved. If you were less than kind, indicate in a couple of words how you defended that behavior—"he had it coming... he's mean to everyone... I put him in his place..."
3. Now indicate "better" or "bitter" next to each for how he or she was affected by your response (did it make him or her more bitter? or a better, higher functioning person?)
4. Not all people return kindness. If you were kind to someone, and he or she did not respond, did you feel angrier toward him or her, or more proud of yourself for being genuine?

Becoming an Agent of Change

We often hear people say, "I can't change the world." This may be true, but what's keeping us from changing *our* individual world? What's keeping us from changing the small world we carry with us when we drive, when we go to our jobs, the supermarket, or live with our families? Ironically, the people who complain the most about others' incivilities are often the most hostile people we meet. At some point all of us have to realize that the world will appear to us in the very manner in which we engage with it. If the world appears rotten, angry, and hostile-we need to remember that it reflects the image we give it.

To disagree, one doesn't have to be disagreeable.

Barry Goldwater

Hostile people are even a little irritated with smiling optimists, because they want everyone to be just as miserable as they are. Hostile people believe that the world is responsible for their misery, just as it should be responsible for their happiness.

The hypocrisy of the complainers and the self-proclaimed "victims" is that their behavior can only add to the hostility in the world. They can't make a shift in their thinking. They are fixated on the problem, which keeps them from creating solutions. We should never forget that we are the creators of kindness; it doesn't appear out of thin air. In all that we do, we either build humanity or tear it down. The following is an eloquent summary of this philosophy that Abraham Maslow shared in 1970.

"Let people realize that every time they threaten someone,

or humiliate, or hurt unnecessarily, or dominate, or reject another human being, they become forces for the creation of psychopathology, even if these be small forces.

Let them recognize that everyone who is kind, helpful, decent, psychologically democratic, affectionate, and warm, is a psychotherapeutic force, even though a small one."

We must also remember that there is potential for this wisdom in children, and it goes back to the example of the child selling candy bars. He was a "psychotherapeutic force, even though a small one."

When we get out of bed in the morning, we have the opportunity to view each moment with either openness or hypersensitivity. By being hypersensitive, we lose our flexibility and optimism. It's like the customers who scream at the waitress for the speck of dirt on a fork. They shouldn't flatter themselves by believing that the waitress secretly plotted with the dishwasher who secretly plotted with the busboy who secretly plotted with the manager to give them a fork with a spot on it for the sole purpose of ruining their day. Chances are in our lifetime we will have a lot of spots on our forks and drinking glasses—we need to get used to it, it's not a conspiracy.

We shouldn't flatter ourselves into believing that the rest of the world is concerned about or responsible for making sure our life proceeds flawlessly—we have to learn to put up with an imperfect world. When we demand a world that perfectly meets our needs, it forces us to interpret others' behaviors as threats. It's no wonder we become miserable.

The effect of our behavior on children is overwhelming, and we shouldn't wonder why they are throwing themselves on the floor in a fit of rage when they see us acting the same as they do...and pitching a fit at the store clerk. They saw it work for us (at least they believe it works for us), and they are merely using the same tactic on us.

Children learn only from the information that is available to them. I had a client who told me about an abusive relationship that took her years to get out of. She said she finally understood abuse when it trickled down to her children. She said, "I think it was the hardest lesson I ever learned, and perhaps the most painful. In the end, however it was also the best lesson I ever learned. At one time, my former husband and I shared a common belief—that he was not a violent person. Our definition of violence was limited—like many others'—to using guns, knives, and fists. Pretty much all other behaviors were nonviolent. He even did fundraising for battered women."

She described how for years he would scream and call her a "bitch" when he was upset, throw tantrums, deny her the right to go places, and not let her access the family funds. Since he didn't hit her, she didn't consider it violence. Until of course, she began acting like other victims of violence—she became depressed and withdrawn. The moment of truth came when she realized that her children began to treat each other, and her in this manner. One day when she told her fourteen year-old to clean his room, he turned to her and used his father's favorite line, "go make me a sandwich, bitch." She described how she fell in a heap and sobbed.

In the end, her husband refused counseling and moved out, but she concluded, "It's been the most difficult time of my life, but I've realized that peace comes at a tremendous cost. While life has been difficult, it's now the most peaceful time of my life for me and my children."

When our children become rude, we can deduce that they drew a conclusion about how to treat others based on the information available to them. What we often fail to understand is the long-term toll that this takes on our relationships.

46

Every relationship, as we know it, changes every day.

None of us has relationships that improve in our absence. The other person may improve in our absence, but no "relationship" improves in our absence, it's impossible. All relationships require some behavior to cause them to change. Every time we are sensitive to others' needs, the relationship changes, and consequently every time we are insensitive, it changes as well.

For example have you ever heard someone say, "My mother knows how much I love her."

"But isn't it true that you haven't talked to her in six months?"

"Yes, but she knows how much I love her."

My question is—how in heaven's name does she know this?

With each day that passes, our relationships either grow or disintegrate. When our children go to bed, the only way that they will have more love is if we gave them more love today.

We never hear people at funerals saying, "I hadn't called her for a year, but I don't regret it; she knew every day exactly how I felt about her."

Did you ever wonder why some people tend to write more, call more, and e-mail more as they grow older? It's because they "get it," they understand life and relationships. Sadly, for some of us it takes a lifetime to "get it." I see parents destroying their connections with their children and never wondering how it's affecting the child. They wonder why the children are afraid to make mistakes around them, come to them for help, or confide in them when life is rough. It's because in time, the little moments of neglect, fits of anger, and assorted moments of disrespect take their toll.

I hear parents say, "I tell my children that they can come to me for anything!" Why would they? They are often scared to death to admit their human flaws to someone who will judge them. The healthiest parent-child relationships have common ingredients, they are always growing, and neither party is afraid to apologize or admit fault.

One-minute reflection: Closeness

List the five people with whom you had the most contact today.

1. Next to their names, place a + mark if you believe that when the day was over, he or she was closer to you and a – if you believe that there was more distance between you when the day ended.
2. Now ask yourself what you would like to put next to each name tomorrow. If you are not interested in a +, why not? What need is being served?
3. Now list one thing you could do (not one that that you believe he or she could do, but what you could do) tomorrow to enhance or ensure your chances to put a + next to that name.
4. Name the top ten most important people in your life (living close to you or far away). If today was your last day on earth, how would you evaluate the number of + or – days you had with them in the last six months?

Civility or Incivility
A Matter of Choices Not Chances

> **Live so that when your children think of fairness, caring, and integrity, they think of you.**
>
> **H. Jackson Browne**

No human is born with meanness, spitefulness, or harshness in his or her personality. These are dysfunctional relational behaviors that are learned. They don't occur overnight, and the only thing that can come out of us is what's inside. Sometimes we can trace these back to a childhood origin, but for the most part they are conscious decisions that we make every day of our lives.

When we see adults who are obnoxious, short-fused, and abusive, we can only assume that they use these behaviors because they work! If they are no longer reinforced for these behaviors, they will no longer work.

Some time ago I went out to dinner with some friends, and I watched a man in our group become hostile with the waitress who was waiting on our table. He sat at our table snapping his fingers and waving at the waitress until she finally came over to our table. The young girl was about seventeen years old and had a "Trainee" badge with her name—"Amy."

"Miss, it just occurred to me that we did not receive our appetizer."

"Oh, I'm so sorry sir, I'll bring it right away…"

"No, no, no…this is just wrong! It's easy to see you have no idea what you are doing and have no idea that the appetizer always comes before the main dish!"

"I'm sorry sir and I know…"

"Let me tell you what you know! You are going to go get the manager right now because I want the appetizer *and* I want it complimentary on my bill!"

By this time the manager had arrived and tried desperately to deal with the irate gentleman (a word loosely used in this case). While the rest of us at the table were shrinking and hiding behind our napkins, the manager assured our table that it would all turn out okay. When it was all over, the irate guest at our table turned to us and smirked saying, "See what you can get when you stand up for your rights?"

Unfortunately, he had confused the difference between the "right to speak one's mind," and the "right to be a jerk." In the end, he was an educator, and he taught some lessons to all those around him:

—The young woman learned that the world is full of jerks.

—The manager learned that the world is full of jerks.

—The people at the surrounding tables learned that the world is full of jerks.

—The people at our table learned that food doesn't digest well when you dine with a jerk.

The day after this incident, I witnessed another loose cannon in a public facility (but in a much smaller and innocent form). This time it was in a bookstore (a very large one—the type that has about a million books and covers an entire city block). When I walked in the front door, I immediately heard the piercing scream of someone who was not getting his needs met. His voice was so loud that it could be heard in all four corners of the monstrous store. His name was "Jamie," he stood about two and a half feet tall and probably had a vocabulary of about fifty words. Everyone in the store heard five of those words over and over and over. "Please! Please Momma, Please! I wanna boook!"

His mother stood in line and did everything that an effective parent should do. She had a choice, like all parents do—should she finish the task that she came here for, or haul Jamie out to the car? Anyone who has had children at this age knows that there are times when we have to bypass the ego and get the job done—no matter how much they scream. Nonetheless, she did exactly what an effective parent should do—**not give in.** Let him scream, and let him scream, and let him scream. Just remain calm and don't give in. And Jamie did scream.

Soon he had regressed and had thrown himself on the ground and continued to repeat his plea of "pleeeease, Mommy…" As he did this, his mother continued to do the right thing. She was calm, collected, and spoke in a soft "broken record" voice. "No, we are not getting the book today…No, we are not getting the book today… No…"

The more he threw a fit, the calmer she remained. The mother had no ego, no need to give in, no need to feel embarrassed, and soon she was on her way. She did not have to scream at him, beat him, spank him, or punish him. She patiently taught him a lesson—that pitching a fit does not work. It's a guarantee that the child either cried himself to sleep in his car seat or simply got over it within the next thirty minutes. But again, a lesson was taught—you can't have everything just because you pitch a fit.

This story is an example of a turning point where we may fail or succeed as parents. Some parents would have given in, because their egos were at stake. There are times when a child has to be removed from a movie theater, a church, or a place where he or she is disturbing others. In all cases—whether you stay or go, the lesson needs to be the same—pitching a fit does not work. What is clear from what we know in educational psychology is that after repeated "pitching a fit" instances, the child will learn that this doesn't work.

In comparison, we have to wonder about the adult in the restaurant. It wouldn't take a rocket scientist to figure out how he arrived at the obnoxious personality he now possesses. Somehow, along the way he discovered a tool for getting his needs met because someone kept giving in to his screaming fits. Consequently, they have now continued well into adulthood. Since this behavior worked—he stuck with it. I've often thought that it would be fun if we could use the same techniques on adults. Imagine if "Amy the Trainee" waitress, had used the calm "broken record technique" on the irate man in the restaurant, "Sir, if you don't want to eat your appetizer, you can leave now... Sir, if you don't want to eat your appetizer, you can leave now...Sir, if you..."

If she would have done that, I'm sure that he would have cried himself to sleep in his car seat too!

> **Neurotic perfectionism has never built a perfect or a productive life. It's much better to be happy and to admit our faults.**

Striving to exercise civility doesn't mean that we are held to a standard of leading a perfect life. Civility is not perfection; it's awareness and work toward progress. Sometimes civil people make mistakes and offend others; the difference is that they have genuine apologies that follow.

Civility is a lifelong ongoing quest. Anytime we find ourselves giving up in our efforts toward it, we've given up hope, and we become jaded. A jaded adult is the world's worst teacher for a child.

It doesn't cost us a nickel to carry a smile. It won't cost us a week's salary if we have a kind word, hold open a door, or apologize when we are wrong. We can create goodness from the resources we already possess, and they may be the most valuable resources we ever know.

One-minute Reflection: Your Grade

As you examine your week, try to describe in a couple of sentences what an absolutely perfect week would look like. This would include perfect civility and flawless behavior.

1. Using the week you describe above as an A+ grade, describe what a B+ day would look like. Can you still pat yourself on your back after a B+ day, or do you dwell on the imperfections?
2. If you have a C day, can you have an A day to balance out the week?
3. What grade could you be satisfied with for the period of a week, month, or year? Where are you at now, and where do you expect to be in six months?

A Healthy Conscience is Our Key to a Life Filled With Caring Relationships

> **No one has yet realized the wealth of sympathy, the kindness, and the generosity hidden in the soul of a child. The effort of every true education should be to unlock that treasure.**
>
> **Emma Goldman**

Some time ago I was standing in a café court in a mall waiting for my turn when a woman in line turned around and suddenly spilled her entire tray of food. Splat! Her fries, shake, and sandwich went tumbling. A child (who looked to be about five years old) rushed over and began to help her pick up the mess as the adults stood and watched. The little boy was not her child; he was merely waiting in the front of the line with his father.

It occurred to me that as adults we have grown so mistrustful that we often pause and ask ourselves—should I help? Here was this child who moved like a bolt of lightning to come to the aid of a stranger simply because it was an extension of his genuine good will. I can understand being cautious when a stranger speaks to me on the way to my car in the middle of the night, but here was a situation where so many adults were slow to jump in to help. What did we have to lose? What would happen to us if we helped? Would we make ourselves vulnerable? Overextend ourselves? Be taken advantage of? Or, perhaps, worst of all, lose our sacred place in line?

I couldn't wipe the smile off my face as I listened to the little boy's conversation as he helped; he not only was a miniature saint, he offered words of wisdom! "You know if you go back to the counter, the man will give you another drink and food, it happens to me all the time."

I thought about that situation and the genuine conscience that the child possessed. He showed empathy—as though he was saying, "Hey, I've been there, I know how it feels!" It also made me think about when someone is struggling with a package, or a door and how some people immediately respond and others don't. It's like we have these little bubbles around us when we are in public that say—*don't step inside mine!*

Most of us appreciate someone holding a door open for us, a courteous smile, or the help of another for something as simple as asking directions. It's a natural warmth that nearly all humans are born with. Sadly however, it's also a human quality that is slipping away. In our fast-lane, "gotta have it now!" and "gotta have it my way!" world, we are overlooking the most precious commodity on the planet—human spirit.

Parents and teachers are increasingly recognizing the "lack of conscience" as one of our greatest concerns for our children. A recent article in the paper detailed how a couple of teenagers methodically tortured a number of animals in an upper-middle-class neighborhood. They captured neighborhood cats and dogs. Together they burned, skinned, sliced, and tortured the animals until they died.

When we think of the heart of a child helping a stranger in the mall, and compare it to the heartlessness of animal torture, we need to examine the influential factors in our culture that can produce one or the other. We are naturally adept to loving relationships, but it's impossible for these relationships to grow if they are not nurtured with other humans.

When we become consumed with only our own needs, our vision is limited. We fail to see how small acts of looking the other way, abrupt exchanges, and impulsive responses can add up to produce a jaded attitude toward the world. We begin to lose faith in the goodness of humankind. The child in the previous story is an example of how a small spirit can make a difference in a person's life in just a matter of seconds. All of us yearn for a world that could operate under such conditions all the time. What we fail to realize is how many hundreds of opportunities we have to touch others every day. Acting on those opportunities is an extension of a strong conscience.

In many ways, talking about civility before talking about conscience is like putting the cart before the horse. We may wonder, "Don't we need to have a conscience before we can exercise civility?" The answer is this—the two act together, and each of them strengthens the other. We think and we behave simultaneously, therefore we must teach behaviors *and* a guiding philosophy at the same time.

A conscience is a guiding philosophy toward life that has the ability mentally to process the good will of our actions. If the world had a strong conscience, we would all stop hurting one another because our behaviors would always have consideration for others' feelings. To have a conscience means that one is motivated by a sense of values and morals. Empathy and ethics become a mere extension of a person who has a strong conscience.

I am often asked, "Can we teach someone to care?" The answer is yes, we can, and **not** caring (or, becoming apathetic) is also a learned process. Our nature is to form relationships, regardless of whether the relationship lasts a few seconds or a lifetime. When we exchange pleasant small talk with the clerk at a counter or remain married to someone for decades, we are acting out of a motivation to care for our fellow humans.

As we examine the prospect of *teaching someone to care,* we know that most humans are born into a healthy connection with others. During the course of their lives, the average person will continually nurture this compassion with others. Somewhere between the child who helped at the mall and the teenagers torturing animals are a number of life lessons that influence a frame of mind in regard to hurting or helping others.

We live in a world where a lot of the "bad guys" are claiming the headlines. Even the strongest among us are susceptible to an occasional belief that the world is made up of nothing but hurtful people. What we fail to remember is that for every terrorist, sniper, racist, and serial killer that there are literally thousands who outnumber them. There are millions more who wake up everyday and hug their children, help their neighbors, and support their friends. The average person will cross paths with hundreds of people every day who want good things for others.

All of us are capable of having momentary lapses in our ability to care for others; and the key is to stop and catch ourselves. When we have a busy day, we may not see the co-worker stressing out, or we may not recognize that our children are down in the dumps because we are so busy with our own lives.

Creating a conscience in children, and maintaining a conscience in adults is nothing more than creating healthy habits of thought. We need to care more for the people in our lives than "today's task." Everyday we see ineffective leaders losing their senses of conscience and empathy. Parents are losing conscience because they are spending more time trying to own everything they see on TV instead of nurturing a lifelong relationship with their children. Teachers are losing conscience because they are now pressured by politicians to "get higher scores," instead of "getting ready for life." Bosses, administrators, and those in positions of power have become seduced by a cultural value that prizes output and productivity over human feelings.

Having a conscience literally saves human lives. It makes our world safer and allows us to live longer. Intelligent children are writing suicide notes to say that they couldn't live up to this world's expectations. What they failed to learn in all of their schooling and family life was that the sacredness of their own lives was the most important issue of all. The solution to developing more conscience in ourselves and in our children is to pay attention to the dysfunctional trends that we have come to accept as normative behavior. We have to pay attention to what's not working as well as what is working.

This chapter will look at the habits and trends that feed the growing "loss of conscience" that we are feeling in today's world. It will also look at how we can promote and influence conscience in others. First, we need to **overcome the myth of "Getting Even."** There is perhaps no other habit of thinking that is more destructive than to believe that "others need to feel my pain." We also need to **understand the difference between healthy and unhealthy guilt**. The chapter will separate how some guilt emerges from empathy and genuine caring, while other guilt serves no purpose other than to make us toss and turn all night. By developing a strong conscience, our moments of guilt will serve us to change behavior and "get it right" in our relationships.

We also need to look how **our egos can create false pride**. In order to enjoy life, we need to laugh at all of the little things. The chapter will look at how we lose our conscience when we develop a habit of "lashing out loud" instead of "laughing out loud" when life doesn't proceed perfectly. A healthy conscience allows us to drop the shields that protect our fragile egos.

Losing our sense of conscience can also be contagious. We need to create an immunity from joining the jaded "I don't care" crowd. If we've joined the crowd that doesn't care, we won't have to look far to see where our children are learning their behavior.

We also lose our sense of caring when we haven't learned to **let go of the past**. It does us no good to harbor resentment. The chapter will also examine how we can avoid poisoning ourselves by learning the skill of "letting go."

Last, the chapter will look at how we are losing our sense of mutual compassion by **clinging to the "need to be right."** If one person must win, the relationship will lose. The need to be right is an outgrowth of the need to control. Our sense of care for others will grow if we can release our egos from this motivation.

If we want to develop conscience, it takes work. Sometimes it's slow, but what could be more important than promoting care and compassion toward others?

The Myth of "Getting Even"

> **Kindness is loving people more than they deserve.**
>
> **Joseph Joubert**

One of the greatest errors in human thinking is in the need to "get even." It's as though we've created a belief that nature will be balanced and a better world will emerge if *the person who caused me pain* can *experience my pain.* "Getting even" is a concept that at times can become an obsession. Those obsessed with "getting even" have lost their interest in helping, nurturing, or trying to guide someone toward kindness. They are consumed with the intent to experience a twisted sense of joy in another's pain.

We hear these obsessions on a daily basis. For many, it becomes *modus operandi* immediately to gravitate to these thoughts, when in reality they know that absolutely no "good" could come from this outcome. We have to ask ourselves—how did we arrive at these habits of thinking? When cut off in traffic, why would a person think, "I'd love to see that road rager wrapped around a telephone pole down the road!"

When crossed by a fellow employee, or boss, why would a person think "I'm going to relish the day that creep gets fired!"

When a criminal commits some heinous crime, what makes us think that 30 lashes will change his or her behavior?

If we examine the most miserable people we know, we will find that they seem to spend most of their days in hypersensitive states ready to pounce on any perceived threat. They run around constantly saying to themselves—"Once they get theirs, I'll be happy!"

They love to imagine that somehow this person who crossed them will get punished and feel miserable—"You made my life miserable, so I would love to see you more miserable!"

We have to ask ourselves—what kind of outcome do we want for humankind? Do we want others to develop more cruelty? Or, do we want them to become more kind? We have to be careful in how we answer these questions because they will determine whether we still have faith in the goodness of others, or if we've given up. Common sense will tell us that it's illogical to be obsessed with "getting even." There's no need to punish miserable people—the punishment is already built in. They spend their days in self-inflicted misery and self-punishment. Why add to it? Couldn't our energy and efforts be better utilized in trying to get more goodness than meanness out of them?

Several years ago when I was attending graduate school, I rented an apartment with my wife and two children. On a Saturday morning I answered the knocking at my door to see my neighbor standing with a chain-saw in his hand. He was very polite as he asked "Would you mind if I started my chain saw at 4:00 in the morning?"

I figured that he must have an important reason so I said, "Sure! You must have a big job to do. Do you need any help?"

He replied, "Actually, I only have a couple of tree branches to cut up, but the real reason that I want to do it is because my damned neighbor behind me keeps mowing his lawn at 10:00 at night; I'll give that idiot some noise! It'll teach him to mow so late!"

After he walked away, I wondered how long he must have stewed over this problem of the late-night mowing, and how long it took him to concoct his plan of justice. I also knew that the late-night mowing was a result of this particular neighbor's late hours of working. It was the only time he could do it.

I also wondered why my neighbor thought that his response would solve anything. Did he expect his irrational act to cause the neighbor suddenly to figure things out? As though the neighbor would think, *Hearing that chain-saw is like a divine message—wow! How could I have ever known that my late night mowing would cause others to chain-saw at 4 a.m.? I've got to thank my chain-sawing neighbor for being so forthcoming in his communication of his needs!*

I found myself shaking my head wondering if this was the beginning of the Hatfields and McCoys feud. I began to think about how often we automatically view the little things in life as threats and feel like we have to fight back rather than seek a solution. It's as though we believe that others' oversights are designed to make us miserable. In this case both of these neighbors were good people, but a failure to communicate could result in an all-out war.

As I think about my former neighbor, it doesn't surprise me to see how prevalent this thinking really is. Not long ago I interviewed a group of sixth graders and asked them for a couple of things. First, I asked them how we should treat others on the playground. Their responses were almost unanimous—nearly every child said, "Treat others the way you would like to be treated." Then I asked them for solutions on how to deal with bullies on the playground. Over half of the children made some remark about "getting back," "getting even," or "hitting back."

Some parents even teach their children always to hit back. The sad reality however is that we know that 80% of the children who are bullied happen to be least able to defend themselves. For some children, hitting back teaches the bully not to mess with them, but does it teach the bully to be kind? The answer is obvious—it teaches the bully to find a more vulnerable target.

We also know that in the majority of instances where children are bringing lethal weapons to school with the intent to cause harm, their most common rationale is to "get back," or "get revenge," on someone. All we have to do is look at the sad state of the world to see the rationale of most of the terrorists. They are also espousing their need to "get back," or "get revenge," on someone. They simply don't want peace.

We are the only creatures who methodically plot to get even with one another. My housecat, Squeaker, doesn't sit around thinking, "as soon as that dog goes to sleep I'm going to ambush him and tear his ears off!" She simply finds a way to live cooperatively with the dog as they respect each other's territory. Of course, with humans being the smart ones in this equation, it's important for us to keep them apart if we suspect that they may fight. We don't sit around with Squeaker and plot to beat up the dog so that she will feel that justice has been done.

If we create healthy habits of thinking, we will promote understanding, not "getting the best of someone," or "getting even." Each time a child spills his or her milk, we need to empathize. When we were children, we all spilled our milk and made messes, but chances are we didn't do it to make someone miserable. Yet, many of us remember hearing, "there you go again—trying to ruin my dinner!" We hear this more often than, "Stevie, at this table we need to pay attention to what we are reaching for in order to avoid messes like this." The child already feels bad enough, and if we are projecting our own insecurities into our responses, we are lashing out in anger instead of understanding.

We can begin to break the habits of aggression and grab two rags to clean up the mess, one for ourselves and one for the child. If we want the child to grow up to be kind, thoughtful helpers, then we need to demonstrate how early on. If we don't, the result is obvious—children grow into the hypervigilant "on guard" defensive creatures that most us despise. As Gandhi said,

"If you love peace, then hate injustice, hate tyranny, hate greed—but hate these things in yourself, not in another."

Teaching children to "get even," is telling them to take the law into their own hands. As adults, if we are punching out the guy who jumped in line in front of us at the theater, we are arrested! We should be! We know that we need to assert ourselves verbally, but not physically. The greatest loss in this lesson, however, is the loss of human conscience. "Getting even," throws conscience and understanding out the window and does nothing more than support the continued use of aggression to solve our problems. It's one thing to defend ourselves; it's another to encourage a child to exact punishment on others.

If we believe in a democratic system of justice, then we will support the law, our courts, conflict resolution techniques, peer mediation, and appropriate skills to solve our problems in our relationships. Children steered toward creating "evenness" instead of "getting even" will have healthier lifelong relationships with their families, peers, co-workers, and life partners.

One-Minute Reflection: Getting Even

Think back to the past few days when you felt you were "done wrong" or "unfairly hurt" by someone's actions. Write down two or three instances that come to mind.

1. As you recall these instances, describe your immediate reaction and the reactions you had in the hours that followed. Did you grit your teeth? mumble under your breath? lash out at others?
2. How many of the above reactions dwelled on getting even? "I should have said..."
   "I wish that I had said..."
   "The next time I see him, he is in for it!"
3. When you wake up tomorrow, take one minute to think about how you will approach your day. Imagine that someone on the road, in your workplace, or in your circle of friends will "rub you the wrong way." Knowing that you are capable of losing a portion of your day to this distress, ask yourself:

   How much of my personal power and self-worth am I willing to forfeit to this conflict?

   How many minutes of my day do I want to waste on anger and impatience?

   How many minutes of "kind behavior" am I forfeiting so that I am wallowing in misery for someone else's problem?

Develop "Healthy Guilt"

Do not be cruel to others unless you are willing to be responsible for their acts of cruelty later in life.

Hungarian Proverb

Having a conscience can also mean having guilt. We are all capable of experiencing healthy and unhealthy guilt. When we obsess on events that occurred years ago or needlessly torture ourselves about things that we can't change, we are experiencing unhealthy guilt. There is no functional benefit to this type of guilt. We know of people who spend a lifetime immersed in self-inflicted agony about things that cannot be changed or altered. There are however, times that we need to reflect on how our selfishness, impulsiveness, or harsh treatment of others has caused pain, and we need to put our energies into correcting the behavior. Healthy guilt has to do with things we can change and motivating us to change them.

Our biggest obstacle is our ego. Swallowing our pride, accepting our human flaws, and dumping our ridiculous rationalizations have to be our first steps. We also have to remember that guilt is a natural reaction when we compromise what we know to be right and wrong. If you've hurt another human being and you *don't* feel guilt, then you are on your way to a personality disorder.

Much has been written to describe "guilt" as a useless emotion. I would strongly disagree, but I think we need to understand guilt in its proper context. All of us have done stupid things in our youth. If you stole money or lied when you were ten years old, should you feel guilty about that now? Most of us would agree that if you were still feeling guilty you would be a little neurotic. This guilt serves no healthy purpose, and this is where we need to separate out the healthy and the unhealthy guilt. Is there something that can be changed or a wrong that could be righted? If so, then let the guilt move you to a new behavior and put closure on the incident.

Instances of "healthy guilt" are evidence that we have a conscience. If you've had to reflect on an inappropriate behavior, it may move you to changes in the future. It's not all that bad to feel this guilt. We all know grumpy people who could benefit from a lot more healthy guilt.

Years ago, my son was involved in a car wreck. It was an early December morning when we got the dreaded call. I could hear the shaking tear-filled voice on the other end of the line, "Dad, I got in a wreck…"

My sixteen year-old son didn't allow himself enough room to stop, and he slid into the back of another car. It was the first snowfall of the season, and the first time he had driven on slick roads. The news reports indicated that there were dozens of fender benders all over the city, and my son was in one of them. My first reaction was like that of any other parent, and I was relieved to hear that no one was injured. My wife and I flew out the door and in a few minutes arrived at the scene just a few blocks from our home.

The physical damage was minimal with only a few scratches to the bumpers of both cars, but the emotional damage was immense. My son had tears in his eyes and was overwhelmed with emotion. The driver of the other car was a well-dressed middle-aged professional woman standing next to her new car. What we didn't know was the scene that took place before we arrived. We later learned from my sixteen year-old and his friend was that the woman had launched herself into a non-stop profanity-laced tirade.

67

It began with her jumping out of her car and approaching my son's car, "YOU F——— IDIOT! HOW COULD YOU BE SO F——— DUMB! ARE YOU EVEN OLD ENOUGH TO DRIVE THAT F——— CAR?! I'M CALLING THE COPS, AND I HOPE THEY TAKE YOUR F———- LICENSE AWAY!

By the time we arrived, she had screamed at our son for more than fifteen minutes. My son did as he was raised to do—he was polite, courteous, and kept his cool. After the information was exchanged, the woman sped away in anger, but my son was traumatized for the day.

We gave him the responsibility of handling all of the repairs, insurance details, and calls on his own. We sat with him at the kitchen table that night as he called the woman whose car he had run into. During the course of the conversation, we heard him say at least four times, "Thank you for your patience...I appreciate your understanding... I'm so sorry..."

As an adult, I'm ashamed to admit that I had a personal fantasy of putting this woman in her place with a tongue-lashing. It then occurred to me that I would be reacting much like she did, with incivility and aggression, *and* it would be nothing more than a desire to "get even." I also realized that these are not the values that I was trying to teach my son. I was very frustrated that this woman could be so mean to a young man she didn't even know. He is courteous, respectful, thoughtful, and in no way would do anything to hurt anyone in his life. He has had his moments of "acting out" when he would battle with his brother (as most siblings do), but has always been a respectful young man.

As parents we would have loved to intervene, but we wanted our son to take full responsibility. He has to deal with all the good and bad that comes with this world. The next night my son received a call back from the woman. In the course of the conversation, the woman apologized and admitted that she was wrong in her actions. She confessed to being scared herself and revealed to my son how she remembered her first accident and how tough it was on her at the time. The apology seemed genuine, a little late, perhaps motivated out of guilt, but nonetheless it seemed sincere. I realized that a sixteen year-old was the teacher that day and his caring and thoughtful actions had made all the difference in the world. He affected another human being, and even though this smart, educated, middle-aged woman was able to dominate and control another person for a period of time, it was the well-meaning and gentle actions of a teenager that made all the difference. The lesson for our son turned out to be much greater than we ever imagined. He learned that there is meaning and purpose in kind acts. It's so easy to be cruel, but it takes real courage to be peaceful.

At times guilt can be a powerful motivator, but we can't beat guilt out of someone, we can't take a cattle prod and shock guilt out of someone, and we can't demand that others care. The only way to find kindness in the heart of another is to give it to that person. The only way to find a heart is to touch it. In the previous story we see a situation like so many others. It's too easy to act out in anger. It takes a great deal of strength to exercise patience and consideration *especially* when we are challenged with verbal abuse.

Acts of anger have a snowball effect. If we keep acting upon anger with anger, the world will never be the place we desire it to be. In every case where we do this, we are acting irresponsibly. If we want the world to be more responsible, we have to be more responsible and hold ourselves accountable for the final outcome of all our relationships. The sixteen year-old stopped aggression in its tracks and took more responsibility for kindness in this world than the adult with whom he interacted.

If the woman who exercised the rude behavior would be able to act differently the next time she is upset, then the young man's efforts to be respectful would have had a powerful effect on the world. We need to keep faith in our acts of kindness. If we begin to believe that kindness has no purpose, we've accomplished two horrible things—we've lost our faith in humanity, and we've lost faith in our own ability to make the world a better place.

One-Minute Reflection: Guilt

"Distress" in most cases is nothing more than an unsolved problem. On many occasions, we experience distress when we know we are compromising something in our behavior. Recollect two or three recent incidents when you felt a conflict that left a "rotten feeling" in your stomach.

1. Now that some time has passed, how do you reflect on the conflict? If it's still making you miserable, check any of the following that apply to the way you think.
   ___ "Others just need to toughen up and deal with me when I'm like that." (callousness, false bravado to cover up guilt)
   ___ "I'm no different than anyone else; conflicts are a part of life; they'll just have to get used to it." (rationalization to cover up guilt)
   ___ "I'm afraid if I apologize, or try to speak to them, I will make myself vulnerable and just set myself up to get stomped on again." (too much ego at stake)
   ___ "They don't deserve my apology. (false pride)
   ___ "It's easier for me to say nothing, or commiserate with others who agree with me." (insecure)
   ___ "I'm getting used to feeling miserable, I'll just keep doing everything for everybody and keep my mouth shut." (false sense of sainthood, martyrdom)

2. If your guilt is causing you pain, which of the ineffective thoughts above are you willing to relinquish to find peace?

3. If you are willing to relinquish any of the above, what plan do you have to "get it right" in this conflict?

Laughing Out Loud Instead of Lashing Out Loud

> **Each day will present us with numerous moments of minor chaos. We must decide whether we will approach these moments with amusement or hostility.**

"My best teachers are the ones who can laugh at all of the little things that happen during the day," said Joan, an elementary school principal. She argued that the best educators among us are not necessarily the ones who are the smartest or the ones who have all of the information. "I have brilliant teachers who are so uptight, so anal, and so intense that the only thing they will ever teach the kids is how to be neurotic. They scream at them, insult them, and continue to wonder why their jobs are so miserable. They are certain that the children are making them crazy. Then I watch the exact same group of children with a patient, good-humored teacher, and it seems like the teacher is working miracles with them. When I hire teachers, I care less about their academic record and more about their passion, sense of humor, and their ability to have fun in the middle of the chaos. I've watched teachers come in and out of my building for decades. Which ones increase performance? Which ones produce well-balanced children? Which ones do the children work hard for? It's easy—the ones who have the 'Three Roll' philosophy— they roll up their sleeves, roll with the flow, and roll with the punches. Most of all, they aren't afraid of mistakes, and aren't afraid to laugh at themselves."

The principal's description of effective teachers provides a familiar situation. We interact with people everyday who have little empathy and conscience, and the evidence is in their inability to laugh with life. Hostile people share a commonality—they can't laugh at themselves. They can laugh at the expense of others, but never at themselves. We can see where these situations create ineffective working relationships with others and in particular, the loss of connection to children. These people are dangerous when they are placed in a position of authority.

Miserable people experience self-humor as a threat. If they are to laugh with others (perhaps about themselves), they become very uneasy because it makes them vulnerable. They cling to their images in their positions of authority. They have an insecure belief that if they are seen as one of us "normal-neurotics," their images would be tarnished, and they would become less effective leaders.

It doesn't take a research project for us to see the obvious—the happiest people we know are the ones who are *not* constantly on guard. People who are filled with joy are always ready to laugh at the incongruencies that occur during their day.

It is my belief that you cannot deal with the most serious things in the world unless you understand the most amusing.

Winston Churchill

We need to face the fact that children will do things that will disturb us (just as we did to our parents). Most of these behaviors are not on purpose. We have to decide whether we can go with the flow, not personalize each incident, and be ready to see the humor in the situation, instead of doing what a lot of people do—punish the child for being a child.

I remember an instance several years ago that was actually physically painful for me. I was coaching a little league team and showing some of the fundamentals on how to throw a ball. On most teams we all know a child or two who needs a little extra care, a little extra attention, and a little extra time. On our team, we had Jeff. He went by "Jeffy." Jeffy was a coach's dream in many ways; he loved to be there, always smiled, and always had fun. He would bounce into practice with his mitt on the wrong hand, and his hat on sideways, but oh how he loved baseball! He was a joy to work with, but baseball skills were new to him, and he had a lot of trouble throwing a ball. As coaches we decided to give him a little special time during every practice to have some one-on-one instruction.

On this night, I worked with Jeffy. We went to an area away from the rest of the team, and I began to talk to him about the art of throwing a baseball. "Okay Jeffy, here's what we're going to do, grab the ball like this, pull your arm back like this, step your lead foot forward in the direction you are throwing, follow your arm through and let it rip! What do you think Jeffy? Do you think you can do it? Great, are you ready to throw it to me Jeffy?"...Jeffy nods... "Okay Jeffy here we go!"

As I took about three steps away from Jeffy, I suddenly saw stars in front of my eyes. This generally occurs when the human brain has suffered a minor concussion as the result of a small flying trajectory making contact with the back of one's skull. Yes... Jeffy had done precisely as I had asked him; he had thrown the ball with perfect form and plastered me in the back of the head. Whammo!! My baseball cap went flying off, and I was in fact seeing stars. It occurred to me that I was not clear enough in my instructions with Jeffy. Perhaps I should have told him that the proper time to throw the ball was when the person you are throwing to has walked a significant distance, turned around, and held his glove up.

I turned around to walk back to Jeffy with the intent to be more explicit in my directions. When I finally found him through the cluster of stars in front of my face, there he was in all of his "Jeffyness" with both hands covering his face and his bulging eyes peering through the gaps between his fingers. Apparently, when I had turned around, Jeffy decided to practice the throwing motion and the ball had slipped out of his hand. The result was a wayward missile that found my head.

As I staggered toward Jeffy I fell to a knee (which was convenient so I could be face to face with those bulging frightened eyes). The only thing I could do was laugh.

The fact that I was pasted in the back of my head (by accident) and his reaction of shock and embarrassment combined for a memorable moment. To this day, whenever I think about Jeffy, I laugh out loud. In his genuineness, he was trying to be the best Jeffy he could be at the time. It is not my desire to have brain damage, but Jeffy did give me a memory that will last a lifetime.

Many of us have struggled to balance laughter in our day-to-day tasks. Laughing is one of the most life-giving and life-enhancing behaviors we will ever engage in. When we lose our will to laugh, we lose our will to live. The situation with Jeffy illustrates how I had the choice to view my brain damage with humor or anger. Life doesn't always go the way we want, and children will sometimes give us brain damage. We have to remember that Jeffy was not acting with malice—it was simply a mistake. In the end, it resulted in a slapstick moment. A hostile perception could have resulted in an attack of anger toward Jeffy and a small scar on his innocent heart. We need to remember that there are thousands of children who are beaten daily for small errors like Jeffy's baseball.

Hostile people create a hypervigilant perception of life's imperfections. They become so serious that it's impossible for them to enjoy any experience that may be the least bit inconvenient. They become the least helpful and the least caring people in our presence. When we consider all of the relationships we've had in life, chances are, in the most meaningful ones, we were able to laugh with someone, and it served as a bond and a mark of a true friendship. It all comes down to our choices.

Consider the relationships where the laughter slowly burned away and was replaced by complacency, apathy, anger or compulsiveness. Without fail, when laughter goes, so does the relationship. When we see a child who can't laugh and enjoy life, it's a clear sign that he or she has lost this wonderful connection of joy to others.

We need to start by modeling the skill of being able to laugh at ourselves. When we do, we will instantly feel an enormous burden lifted from our shoulders. It allows us to dump our false egos. Self-humor will move us through life's roughest moments, guide us through the tough times, nurture us through the pain, and remind us to not take ourselves so seriously. Humor is also a true sign of maturity. As Ethel Barrymore once said, "You grow up the day you have your first real laugh at yourself."

For all of the pain that many children will endure in their lives, why not place a high priority on a skill that enables them to heal themselves? Besides, there is no other skill that is as fun to model as that of a warm sense of humor. When we dump our ego shields and laugh through the little things in life, we not only form stronger connections in our relationships, we also increase mutual empathic feelings toward one another.

One-Minute Reflection: Laughter

The average adult laughs less than ten times a day. The average child laughs hundreds of times a day. Laughter is the evidence that we are enjoying life. Does this mean that we are enjoying life less as we get older? Shouldn't it be the other way around? Shouldn't we laugh more as we get older because we learn more about how wonderful life really is?

1. How many events in the last week were so significant that you will remember them the rest of your life? (We may have a life-shattering event, but chances are, most weeks in the year will fall into the category of "status quo," made up of everyday tasks, trials, and tribulations.

    Looking ahead to new week, most of us can assume that life will go according to plan but with some flaws. When these flaws occur, how many are the result of "life as normal" with people being themselves, children being children, and you being you?
2. Knowing that life in the coming week will be filled with incongruencies and flaws, what do I anticipate as my reaction to them? Am I content with this type of reaction? How many of life's moments will I respond to on "threat alert" and how many will I respond to on "silly alert?"
3. What are my children and loved ones learning from me based on my reaction to life?

Beware of the Hostility Virus

> **Choose your friends wisely. You go hanging around with those hoodlums, idiots, and mean kids—you'll end up thinking and acting just like them.**
>
> **Mom**

Our mothers were right, we become like those with whom we associate. We know the "perpetually miserable" office clique that thrives on gossip, misery, martyrdom, and a myriad of assorted negative thoughts. We also know that they can be influential.

In all that we do each day, we will affect the world. If we choose to become a model of deviousness and hostility, we can't expect our influence to be any different. We know that we become like those with whom we associate, so we shouldn't wonder if our children are irritating us with behaviors that mirror ours.

A fellow psychologist recently shared with me that his childhood friend had been indicted on a huge scam that involved bilking people out of millions of dollars. He also said, "It doesn't surprise me; he grew up in a home that taught him how to get what you want out of life by being devious."

He said he remembered a time when he and his friend were both ten years old. His mother was speeding when a cop pulled them over. She turned to the boys and said, "Watch what I do with this cop."

By the time that the police officer had arrived at her window, she was already in tears and pleading about problems with her speedometer and gas pedal. In a few short minutes, the cop felt bad for her and decided against issuing a ticket. He said that what he remembered most clearly was his friend and the mother laughing hysterically as they drove away. "They were so proud of how she had manipulated the cop. When I read in the paper last week that he had been arrested for such a devious thing, it didn't surprise me at all. As a boy he learned to live without a conscience."

Every time we compromise our integrity, we need to keep in mind who's watching. Where do we expect our children to get their courtesy, if they are watching us drive and listening to, "You stupid son of a biscuit. Oh, how can anyone be so much of an idiot! Where in the hell did he get his license"? If we are acting out when we are in a line, or in traffic, or inconvenienced, we need to remember who is catching all of those chips that are flying off of our block. Do we want our children to become road ragers? Do we want them to be helpful? Do we want them to give others the benefit of the doubt? Or, view each exchange as a threat?

There are even bigger and more important questions that we need to ask. Do we want them to rescue the kid who's being bullied on the playground? Do we want them to have a happy or miserable view of others? Do we want them to treat their spouse or children in this manner?

They can only behave in a manner that has been modeled to them. Becoming a model of conscience should not merely be a goal for influencing others, but also a goal for the sake of our own. When we lose our integrity, the whole world loses a little bit of its integrity as well. This selfish, hostile defensiveness can do the world absolutely no good. If we want a personal motivation for being a model of conscience, we also have to re-alize that these behaviors shorten lives. We know from research that stressful hostile people have more illnesses, accidents, and relationship problems. Isn't it wonderful to think that we can

pass on a life to our children that will allow them to live not
only longer but also profoundly meaningful lives?

Most Lethal Poisons Come From Within

> **Never waste time obsessing about someone who did you wrong. Every moment you spend whining you could get even is a moment of life wasted. If you must wish for something, wish he will not do others harm.**

Forgiveness is a concept that is often seen as a weakness.
There are numerous definitions, but all of them consist of three
major components. First, forgiveness involves giving up resentment against another. Second, it is also giving up the desire to
punish. Third, forgiveness is to stop being angry. Despite these
definitions, we often see forgiveness as a flaw in one's character.
When we reflect on this simple definition, what could be more
productive than giving up anger, resentment, and a desire to punish?

Our children are taught to harbor anger, and to cling to the
past. Holding on to this anger creates an obsession with the idea
that "if you have given me pain, you need to feel it too." After
tragedies, people are sometimes fixated on the idea that in order
to make changes in the world, we need to remain angry and resentful. Sometimes anger can serve to motivate us toward significant changes, but only if the energy is channeled into productive resolutions. If the anger serves in no positive influence,
then it is only capable of draining our energy.

Others see forgiveness as an ineffective solution because of the belief that the scales of justice were never balanced unless someone felt pain. In either case, we are giving up our personal power, our sense of self-worth, and our integrity every time we refuse to let go of resentment.

To remain angry does nothing to help shape the future of our relationships and the world around us. One of most common themes that I have dealt with in counseling is resentment. Resentment harbors anger like nothing else we know. It also keeps us from thinking clearly about a solution.

I once had a middle-age woman tell me in counseling how she had been miserable for most of her life because of the abuse she suffered as a child. What she failed to realize up until that point was that her anger would never solve anything. There's an old saying about anger that says, "Anger is like poisoning yourself and hoping the other person dies."

I shared this saying with her, and I remember her coming back a week later to tell me that she was tired of poisoning herself. We are not doomed to perpetual anger and resentment, but we are dooming our children to perpetual anger if we are teaching them how to **not** let go. She then recalled how her mother spent years telling her how she was angry at her father.

The woman realized that she learned the habit of "not letting go," from her mother. She also realized how much it was draining every bit of life out of her. The problem with teaching resentment is that we are teaching our children to *not* move on. Forgiveness takes much more courage than resentment. To forgive truly is not about reconciliation, making up with anyone, being friends again, or saying, "What you did is okay." Forgiveness is an internal statement of, "I will never let you take my power from me again." It is the personal decision to let it go. If we can't let it go, then all we are doing is "poisoning ourselves and hoping the other person dies."

It takes conscience to forgive. It's a sense of right and wrong that is on a higher plane than most of our impulsive thinking. To forgive means that we know what is right for ourselves and the world. Making it right doesn't include the violation of others, or the belief that "since I was violated—I have a license to violate."

Children are amazingly flexible creatures who most often do move on; they only learn to obsess on "getting even" when they are around adults who constantly display these behaviors. For some, the lack of forgiveness is an everyday thing. They obsess about the guy on the highway who cut them off. They obsess for two months about something their co-worker said—*I should have said this...* Some people not only obsess about the little perceived injustices, they are lifetime unforgivers! *I'll never forgive Uncle Paul for wrecking my car!*

If we look back on the definition of forgiveness, it is about giving up resentment, giving up punishment, and giving up the anger. If we cling to our stubborn egos, we believe that it's about *giving in*, or *giving up*. True forgiveness is far from giving up; it is the mental skill of moving on. Forgiveness gives us life. Resentment, punishment, and anger take life away, as they are three of the most debilitating habits of thought we will ever know. They induce misery in ourselves and others, and have no positive, constructive purpose.

If we can't model the ability to move on, the only thing our children will be able to do is learn a habit of needlessly obsessing on how they were wronged.

Let Go of the Need to be Right

> **Love is the only force capable of transforming an enemy into a friend. We never rid of an enemy by meeting hate with hate.**
>
> **Martin Luther King**

Those who have the greatest need to be right and the greatest need to win at everything may be the ones among us who also have the weakest egos. They have an armor shield that is constantly on guard. In meetings, decisions, and relationships, they see any disagreement as a personal attack, and they come back with guns-a-blazing.

They sometimes give themselves labels to cover up their obnoxious attacks. *I can't help it...I'm just a perfectionist...assertive...competitive...strong-wi lled...* They use these labels to shield their fragile egos that demand that everyone see it their way. They are difficult to communicate with because they see feedback as attacks from traitors. Even if we try to be gentle and honest with our feedback, they see attacks.

If a child grows up with a parent who has an excessive need to be right, or to win, you can bet that child will soon adopt the same attitude in life. When he or she becomes a teenager, watch out! It doesn't matter what you discuss with him or her, his or her only goal is to win, and the only good word is "the last word."

One woman described to me how she one day realized that no matter what relationship she was in, she had to win every argument. As a result, her personal and professional lives were a series of fragmented relationships. She said her co-workers found her difficult because she couldn't stand to be wrong. She also said that her last five boyfriends all tabbed her as inflexible.

In therapy she began to discover where she learned her patterns of communication. She described a father who never lost an argument, was never wrong, and never apologized. Her father was such a control freak that the children couldn't get out of the house quick enough. As much as she hated to admit it, she was becoming the beast that she described.

An important step we make in our maturity is to recognize the traits we have inherited and decide what path we will take. Obviously, the woman realized that she inherited her inflexibility from her father. As a need to control his own life, he sought to control others in authoritarian relationships. Like many of us who have lived around these ogres, we eventually come to a crossroad. Knowing this, the woman had two possible paths. She could inherit the behavior, defend it, and rationalize it. Or, she could seek new behaviors that would allow her to live with the fact that she is not always right.

Hanging on to false pride is the quickest way to sever our connections with our loved ones, and *especially* with our children. The need to be right keeps us from being loved. Certainly there are situations where our authority is important, and as adults we have to exercise that authority. Children don't need to be missing school or out on the street at 11:00 at night; they don't need to be playing in the streets, and youngsters don't need to have multiple body piercings and tattoos. There are many judgments that we make for children that are common sense and may provide safety.

In their interest however, we need to develop their ability to make decisions and become autonomous. If it's all about adults needing to be right, it's a no-win situation. If we always have to win, we can never fully self-examine, and can never fully let our guards down.

The product of the "I'm always right" philosophy is a child who is frightened of making mistakes. It's not uncommon to see children scream at their own parents when striking out on a little league field. It's no wonder they don't want their parents around. They would rather compete on the sandlot with other children who were understanding, forgiving, and supportive.

One-Minute Reflection: Viruses and Poisons

The viruses and poisons in our lives keep us from having strong mental health. These threats to our mental health come from outside of ourselves as well as from within, and each time we are infected, we become more ill and less effective. Check any of the germ bugs that may have produced a recent illness for you.

___If others disagree, I immediately feel tension.

___When I am at odds with another, I seek out people who are willing to talk about this person, in order to make me feel better.

___Sugar coating and pretend "sweetness" always help me to get what I want in life.

___I just can't hold back when I'm surrounded by chaos; I become chaotic too.

___When a bad person hurts me, I obsess on how great it will be when he gets punished for his behavior.

___When things aren't going my way, I become a thorn in everyone's side.

___When I have to deal with people I can't stand, it's really important for me to win the argument and to be right always.

___It really bugs me when people get away with things I think are wrong.

Any of the above viruses can leave us incapacitated and sick for a period of time. If you marked any of them, go back and review them. If there was one habit of thinking that you could inoculate yourself from for the rest of your life, which would it be? What day-to-day inoculation plan could you incorporate for yourself? Who or what is infecting you on a daily basis?

There is a saying, "We are either affecting others or infecting others in all that we do." Do you do more infecting or affecting with your loved ones? Co-workers? Children?

One of the best gifts we can give others is our conscience. A strong conscience allows us to listen and to understand others' feelings. Without it we cannot be patient, supportive, or forgiving. Our conscience is also the path to understanding our own limitations and flaws. We need to drop the ego and replace it with the vulnerability that allows us to admit our faults and treat others as though our future depends on it. Our future *does* depend on it.

Building a Resilient Personality Provides the Shock Absorbers for Life's Bumpy Road

Resilience is not just surviving life and living to tell about it, it's surviving life and living to laugh about it.

Inventory Your Own Resilience Skills

Remember when we were children and we had to listen to a variety of adults telling us things like, "When I was your age, I had to fight off a pack of wild dogs every day just to get to school... I had to walk 50 miles every day and mend my cuts and bruises with a staple gun! You have no idea how horrible life was! I have no idea how I survived it all!"

Of course we were thinking, *Yes, I do know how horrible life was because you keep telling me! And we **are** wondering why you chose to survive it at all!* We didn't develop a sour attitude out of disrespect—it's just that we got tired of their martyrdom. It seemed like for every story about a hardship, there were a dozen more that could top it. It wasn't the hardship story that bothered us—it was their perspective.

We can also think of adults who described their hardships while they smiled. They smiled about the lessons they learned, the good times, and the relationships. There are survivors among us, and there are survivors who have grown into stronger human beings in the process. There is a huge difference between the two, one has found meaning in the bumps in the road, and the other has found misery.

If you've ever wondered why children don't look forward to being adults, it's because all too often they hear adults telling them how miserable life will be. Why would they want to grow up and become one of these creatures?

Resilience is the ability to make it over life's bumpy roads and still be able to smile. Some time ago I watched a news report about Mother Teresa. She held a starving child in her arms, walked the streets among other starving people, and touched them as she smiled. She seemed fulfilled in her ability to provide comfort in spite of the destitute conditions. The newscast then switched to another story about a group of lawyers who were describing a situation as, "One of the most important issues of our time." They were referring to the unfair fees charged for use of ATM's. Certainly we need to address unfairness, but they spoke of the two-dollar fee as though the apocalypse were upon us. They ranted and raved about the unfairness of life and how these monsters were taking advantage of them!

As we compare the two news stories, it causes us to wonder—what's important in life? Should I be concerned about starvation? How does it stack up against the issue of whether or not my life was ruined because I didn't plan ahead enough to have cash in my pocket? How is it that one person can find meaning in horrible conditions, and others can be miserable while living in affluence? In the span of just a few minutes, the perspectives on life were as different as night and day.

What most of us have to endure isn't really enough to make any of us miserable unless we choose to make it so. When we see people who are happy, we believe that somehow this bliss fell in their lap. We don't as often wonder—what choices are they making that I am not?

All of us have known those people who seem to bounce through life with everything going their way. We've also seen people who wake up each day wondering why they are miserable and why life is such a hard luck experience. Our children are destined for one of the two paths, and the difference is in their personal resilience.

Perhaps the saddest thing we will ever experience is a child who has given up on life. In most cases it is because he or she has not had the opportunity to learn to develop resilience and not been able to experience a relationship with an adult who modeled healthy resilience. Without resilience skills, it's impossible to develop healthy connections to others.

When parents are asked what they want most for their children, they rarely seem to say, "I want my kid to be the…best looking…smartest…richest…most athletic…most popular…" Parents most often say, "I want my kids to be happy." The problem is that many of these parents themselves are not happy, and they are therefore incapable of modeling strong skills in resilience. Every bump in their road is filled with hardships.

A major problem with the concept of resilience in our culture is the way we define it. It's counterproductive and useless to scream at a child with such notions as, "Get tough! Learn to buck up! Don't be such a wimp! You pathetic cry baby!" Some people honestly believe that the harsher we treat others, the more we are doing them a favor. They believe in the myth that resilience is a jaded, rough-tough "to hell with everybody" attitude. Unfortunately, cynicism can only create misery. True resilience creates a positive perspective because it is founded on the belief that life is worth living for its own sake. It is worth living because it has purpose and it has the potential for joy.

Many people have overcome a number of obstacles but seek to wallow in martyrdom. Others can overcome the same obstacles and lead joyful lives. The difference lies in the internal processes we use to view our problems. The single biggest mistake we make in our thinking is to believe that something outside of ourselves is responsible for making us happy. All the tools and all the formulas are within each of us; our task is to nurture the positive ones.

> ## It's not life's obstacles that make us miserable—it's our inability to deal with them.

During our lives we will have struggles cropping up continually. Some we will ease into and others will hit us like a cold punch from behind. We will have conflicts in our jobs, relationships, and families. We will lose loved ones, our health will change, and the world will transform before our eyes. Since struggles and obstacles are a given, what we need to think about is not will life turn out great for me? Rather, we need to focus on how well am I prepared for life when it doesn't flow smoothly? And, am I able to enjoy life when the road gets rough?

The happiest people we know are those who have the strongest skills in resilience. Resilient people and miserable people are distinctly different in their experiences of life. Their behaviors, motivations, and perceptions determine whether or not they will experience joy and fulfillment. If we want to teach resilience to our children as well as those around us, we continually have to develop resilience skills in ourselves.

There are five basic mental competencies that resilient people possess. When we teach the skills of resilience to a child, we are nurturing the aptitude of "bouncing back" when one is challenged. Resilient people don't learn these skills and move on. In fact, the "mental skills" are lifelong exercises that remind a person of who he or she is, what he or she has, and what he or she is becoming.

MENTAL SKILL #1—*CONTENTMENT*

—*Resilient people understand that they already possess all that they need to be happy.* They know that happiness doesn't just happen to someone; it comes from within. They can wake up each day, look in the mirror and say, "I already have everything I need to be happy." They know that many things in life can provide opportunity, such as money, power, and privilege, but they also know that it isn't necessary to have these things to be happy.

MENTAL SKILL #2—*GROWTH*

—*Resilient people are in a constant state of change and growth.* They are forever changing because they are always evolving into new persons. They can say to themselves, "I am not afraid to fail, take risks, and create new choices. I will be open to change and growth everyday." Their healthy sense of confidence is tied to their personal ongoing growth.

MENTAL SKILL #3—*COMPASSION*

—*Resilient people are motivated to improve the quality of their connections to others.* They live for others as much as for themselves. They look at each day saying, "I need to do everything I can today to develop stronger relationships with those around me." This motivation results in a genuine generosity and sense of good will toward *all* others.

MENTAL SKILL #4—*CONTROL*

—*Resilient people exercise personal control.* They see life as welcoming instead of threatening. No matter what happens to them in the course of a day, they can say, "I can rise above, rather than join the insanity around me." When they are challenged, they don't lose control, fall apart, or act out. They develop patience rather than paranoia.

MENTAL SKILL #5—*OPTIMISM*
—*Resilient people see life for its possibilities.* This not only allows them to be encouraging to others, but they are "self-encouraging" as well. They approach all of life's hurdles with the same mantra, "No matter what happens to me today, I'm fairly certain that I can survive—and survive with a smile." Optimism is not only useful for problem solving, it will also reduce stress. The resilient individual always takes the positive road, seeking lessons rather than excuses for self-crippling behavior.

The result of these five qualities is a person who is positive, productive, and altruistic—one who fully realizes that life is far from perfect but who has a number of resources existing to help through the tough times and to understand failure in the larger scheme of life. Miserable people see resilient people either as naïve (because they just don't understand how miserable everyone should be!) or lucky (Damn them! A happy life just fell in their laps!). Raising our children with resiliency skills will guide them to make choices and not to blame chance or luck. Resiliency skills will also enable them to have a much greater chance for strong relationships and personal fulfillment.

MENTAL SKILL #1
— CONTENTMENT

Resilient people understand that they already
possess all that they need to be happy

**Do not let what you cannot do interfere
with what you can do.**

John Wooden

Some people can look upon nearly any situation and find meaning, motivation, and a reason to persevere. Others can spend a lifetime wondering why meaning won't come to them. John Wooden's quote points to part of the formula for misery—stay focused on the things you cannot do!

A news team recently visited one of our local high schools to interview a young man who had just broken some weightlifting records. At seventeen years old, he was an All-American and a World Champion in powerlifting. At about 115 pounds, he could lift three times his body weight. He sat with an ear-to-ear grin and animated hands as he answered question after question.

The biggest part of the story focused on his mental strength. The weight training happened to be one of the easiest challenges in his life. The young man had numerous physical problems. His vision ailments included chorioretinitis, glaucoma, a detached retina, and cataracts which all rendered him legally blind. All things beyond an inch in front of him were a mass of blurs. He was also born with his kneecaps on the side of his legs. During the first few years of his life, he would fall down with out warning. Between those two setbacks, he had a total of eleven surgical procedures. These were minimal problems in comparison to his epilepsy. He had intractable epileptic seizures that struck him like lightning nearly every day of his life. Surgery, dozens of different medications, and hospitalizations never offered a cure for the seizures.

He smiled through the interview and answered every question that came his way. The questions regarding bench pressing, and dead lifts were easy. The questions about his problems seemed to be more difficult to answer, and some seemed to stump him.

The reporter asked "Does it ever bother you to think about all the things that you can't do?"

The young man thought for a moment, searching for the right answer before shrugging his shoulders, "I…guess I haven't…really thought about what I can't do. I suppose I'm just happy for all of the things that I can do."

The interviewer continued to ask about the things that hindered his life, "…but you'll never be able to drive and do many of the other things that kids your age do. You can't see the blackboard in class, reading requires special devices, you have to take a lot of medications for your epilepsy, and the seizures keep coming. I suppose that might get you down sometimes."

The strong young man didn't bat an eye. "I guess I know that there's always someone out there who is worse off than me, so I guess I can't really feel sorry for myself." He smiled as though nothing could stop his good mood.

The tragedy is that we see a tremendous number of children who have a lot more going for them in physical ability and a lot fewer obstacles, but they are disadvantaged in their ability to see life for its potential. They are crippled by a disparaging lack of resilience. Our goal must be to develop our own resilience, then model it, teach it, and reinforce it in those around us.

Resilient people have been able to mature past the "delusion of need" that is prominent in our culture. It's as though we've been trained like Pavlov's dog. Our world conditions us to salivate at every new cellphone, car, DVD player, and piece of clothing on the market. In the tradition of classical conditioning, we see people who are thrilled every time they have the new soft drink, food, or gadget. We keep trying to reward ourselves with these things, and we are teaching our children that these are the things that create true happiness, and that *not* to own them will result in a lack of fulfillment.

Resilient children and adults approach each day knowing that they already have everything they need to be fulfilled. This single quality, itself, creates a person who is a strong problem solver. *Distress*, to the resilient person, is simply an unsolved problem within himself. To the neurotic, distress is a force outside himself that he can blame for all of his crippling behaviors.

As with the high school student weightlifter, his happiness did not depend on something outside of himself, nor was it contingent upon another's scale of happiness. He developed the mental skill of being able to place life's difficulties within a perspective, knowing that the absence of certain physical abilities did not result in misery. Booker T. Washington once said, "I have learned that success is to be measured not so much by the position that one has reached in life as by the obstacles which one has overcome while trying to succeed."

Miserable people seem to be focused on what's missing in their lives, and why life isn't serving them better. People with strong skills in resilience are always focused on moving forward, moving on, and getting mileage out of what they do have.

Our children are listening and watching. We need to be careful about what we are teaching if they are hearing us say, "Life would be wonderful *if only*... I owned that new Mercedes...my stupid boss would drop dead...I could win the lottery...I could

94

meet the right person…" Children will become more resilient if they learn that *"if only"* is false need, and that contentment is the evidence of a true appreciation of life.

One-Minute Reflection: Contentment

For the following items, place a check next to those that apply to you (even if they are only partially true). Check any that have applied to you in the past year.

___The more money and nice things I provide for others (and for myself), the happier we will be.

___When I sit back and reflect on my day, most often I'm thinking more about the problems of my day rather than how thankful I am to have what I have.

___It's the people in my life who are most responsible for the stress I feel.

___If I could double my salary, I would be twice as happy.

___My wish list for life has more possessions on it than desires to be closer to others.

___Happiness in my family is highly dependent on my children having "more." (Some of the "more's" may include more playing time on the soccer field, more hits and fewer strike outs, more A's on the report card, more friends, more popularity, and more wins at beauty pageants and spelling bees.)

Continue with the chapter; we will revisit these items at the end.

MENTAL SKILL #2—GROWTH

Resilient people are in a constant state of change and growth.

"We cannot become what we need to be, remaining what we are."

Max Dupree

Most of us can pick up a photo album and recall a moment in our lives when life seemed perfect. It's as though we wish we could freeze that moment, capture it, and live in it, *and* if we did, then life would be perfect. The reason that this moment seemed so perfect is because at that very moment we were becoming something greater than we were before. We were experiencing life as joyful and fulfilling, and we could feel the best part of us emerging from our personality.

We know that it's impossible for life to be a string of blissful events, but at the same time we know that for many of us, these moments are becoming fewer and fewer as life goes on. We know that life is forever changing, and some of us fight it like it was the plague. In regard to *change*, it all comes down to this simple concept—we either change and grow into something more beautiful each day, or we change and deteriorate into something less each day. With each moment of our lives, we are taking in information and trying to navigate through life's struggles; we are becoming something different than we were five minutes ago.

Look at some of the people you have known for the last five years. For each one of them you could make some comment on his or her change, "She seems happier, he seems more content.

She seems more bitter, he seems more selfish." Even for the people of whom we say, "They haven't changed." chances are they are more than what they were before. You can't be the same old jerk for the last twenty years, without losing something in life, and you can't be the same old wonderful person for the last twenty years, without gaining more love and respect.

The world will always change, our relationships will grow, and life will move forward. If you feel more miserable now than you were two years ago, it's because you don't have the tools to deal with the changes in your life. Also remember that if you are becoming more miserable, then you are also a miserable force for those in your life. True resilience is the ability to emerge past life's challenges with more joy. It is the ability to find growth in all stages and phases of life.

As we get older, life hands us more responsibility, and it demands more accountability. Life requires courage in order to deal with change. If we fail to develop this responsibility, the result is what's known as the FRISC recipe, characterized by at least one of the following five ingredients (and most often more than one): **Facades**—allows one to never be seen without his shield. To let down one's guard and be human (laugh and cry with others) would be too much for the recipe, (and one's ego) to handle. **Rigidity or Regimentation**—helps create a low tolerance for mistakes and differences of opinions in others; will also tolerate only your routine and status quo. **Infallibility**—there's no need ever to admit fault or apologize. **Suspiciousness**—this will allow the creation to maintain an obsession with "loyalty" because of an intense fear of personal rejection. Last but not least, top off with a layer of **Control**—if you feel out of control on the inside, you can compensate by trying to control more people and things on the outside.

Any of the ingredients listed above can be a symptom of a fear of change. It takes courage to move beyond these characteristics to decide that our growth is more important than our pride. Ambrose Redman once said, "Courage is not the absence of fear, but rather the judgment that something else is more important than fear." We all know people who can't apologize, even when they know they are wrong. When we apologize to another person, whether it is a family member, a friend, co-worker, or a child, we are saying, "Our relationship is more important than my pride." We have made a "judgment that something else is more important than fear."

Resilient adults and children are constantly developing layers of confidence that allow them to welcome change and lose their fears. By being open and flexible with children, we are teaching them the same. If they lose their rigidity, they can become more confident in virtually every aspect of their lives, from answering questions in class to making new friends.

There are pivotal points in most of our lives that either cause us to have faith in our growth, or to give up on it and accept the status quo. I once knew a professional who had a great deal of responsibility as an administrator at a college. When he started in his position, almost all of the people who worked for him thought he was a jerk. He was short-tempered, inconsiderate, and a well-rounded tyrant. Several years later, everyone who worked for him thought he was much more reasonable. I had a casual discussion with him about aging, and he shared with me that he liked himself more now than he ever had. He talked about how hard it was to swallow his "humility pill." He said that his first wake-up call was from a kind secretary who came into his office and said she was quitting. He described his encounter with her, "She told me that she believed I was the loneliest person she had ever met. She also told me that I was unapproachable and that I saw disagreements as disloyalties. In some ways it was some of the most difficult feedback I had ever received. Here I was believing that the *product* and the *output* in our institute were the most important things in life. In the process I was using people as doormats, and I was building walls between us.

"I felt like I got hit with a brick over my head when my secretary said, 'do you realize that in the two years we've worked together, you've never asked anyone in this office—how are you? How is your family? How was your weekend? Do you realize how your little sarcastic comments hurt us? Do you also realize that you have made mistakes and never admitted them?'

"At first I was mad, defensive, and I made excuses in my head why I had to act that way, but then I got scared. I really did feel lonely. I was afraid that if I was human people would reject me. You know what's the best lesson I learned?—That if I was neurotic, scared, apologetic, and just me—then people actually became nicer, and more open to me. I also discovered an amazing thing—people work harder in relationships when they feel closer, *not* when they feel more threatened."

There were several profound lessons that this administrator experienced that are key elements in growth and resilience. These lessons for growth are the same for adults or children. First, we need to learn that life will be filled with rejection and failures. Secondly, we need to realize that we isolate ourselves when we act out with revenge or pettiness (in regard to feeling rejection). And third, when we are connected to others, they are more likely to feel indebted to us.

People who come across as threatening are often very insecure and fearful of change. Teachers and parents who want to rule with intimidation and fear are the ones who are most intimidated and fearful of losing control.

If we are constantly aware of change and growth, we will more easily be able to get up when we are knocked down. Each time a resilient person can "get up off the canvas" he or she is a little

> **It's not whether you get knocked down,**
> **it's whether you get up.**
>
> **Vince Lombardi**

more reflective and insightful. We have the choice to lie on the ground in a state of anger and defensiveness, or we can get back up. A person choosing anger will stay down and will grumble at life. Getting up is choosing to let go of the anger and create a plan to stay standing.

Failure is also a given in life's scheme. Avoiding failure in life doesn't mean one has had success. Resilient people have just as many failures as gloomy people (sometimes more). The difference is in how they bounce back; gloomy people don't bounce back. Gloomy peple lose their faith in their ability to grow and change with life's challenges.

Children who are giving up on their ability to grow can only deal with life's setbacks in one of two ways: they succumb to failure and give up on life (apathy), or they get back at life (aggression). Either one of these reactions in its most extreme form will result in instances that we hear about in the news. When these children are overwhelmed, they go to extremes—and on shooting sprees. If they act out, the shooting spree is turned outwards as aggression. If they give up, the shooting spree is turned inwards as suicide.

In order to grow as individuals, we must keep an ear open for feedback. Resilient people not only welcome feedback, they use it to make personal changes. Ineffective leaders and parents always fear feedback. As with the college administrator, it took courage to face the feedback from another person, and even greater courage to begin to make the small changes.

Our growth depends on our ability to develop layers of resources. If we can't solve a problem on our own, we need to reach out to the next level of resource. Our will to grow will cause us to reach out to books, friends, and professional resources. We need to become vulnerable and continue to seek out resources until we solve the problem. By developing our own resiliency, we become a layer of resource in other people's lives. We need to make ourselves the best resource that children have, become the strongest layer of resource that they can depend upon in all situations.

A body of research suggests that the most troubled children are those who have had to rely only on their own resources to raise themselves. If left only to their own resources (without healthy connections to healthy adults), it is impossible for children to prosper. If we look at the most deviant children in recent history, the commonality is the same—they lacked the resources to solve their problems and lashed out at others.

We can promote resiliency in children (and in our loved ones) by modeling vulnerability and receptivity to our mistakes. Besides, always being right and incapable of error is unrealistic. We may fool children for a while, but eventually they will see through us.

People who have stopped reaching out have a common saying, "that's the way it's always been done." It's like saying "an outhouse in my back yard is better than plumbing...I should take a horse to work...do my homework by candlelight...use a quill pen to write that paper...." *Why?* *"Because, that's the way it's always been done."*

Change is a lifetime process and a way of life for strong people. They see "change" as the key to happiness rather than "luck." We need to build layers of personal resources that allow us to filter the world's feedback. In doing so, we are modeling to our children how to make themselves vulnerable so they are not afraid of change. Healthy change is impossible without an open heart.

One-Minute Reflection: Growth

For the following items, place a check next to those that apply to you (even if they are only partially true). Check any that have applied to you in the past year.

___Often I rely on others' approval to be happy.

___I'm not as happy as I used to be. The more complicated that life becomes, the more difficult it is to find joy.

___Bad things seem to happen to me more than the average person.

___People tend to think of me as a person who is very "set in my ways."

___I'm more bored now than I ever have been; sometimes I feel like life has reached a plateau for me.

___I'm happiest when life is very routine. It's important for me to have most of my day go without flaws, failures, and setbacks.

Continue with the chapter; we will revisit these items at the end.

MENTAL SKILL #3—COMPASSION

Resilient people are motivated to improve the quality of their connections to others.

> **If the solution to the problem only benefits one person, it was never a solution to begin with.**

Strong, compassionate people live by a humanistic ethical philosophy. In other words, they live for others as much as for themselves. This sense of ethics is not a defined set of rules. When a person treats another human being with genuine kindness (the kind that comes from the heart), this is the highest form of humane ethical behavior. Ethical behavior cannot be reduced to a set of do's and don'ts, because the best that can happen is an idea laced with gray areas. An ethical person sees all other lives as important. All behavior toward others will be activated from this single philosophical belief.

There are hundreds of codes of ethics from many professional organizations that outline appropriate and inappropriate behaviors. These are important for our professions, but in the end, if any behavior benefits an individual at the expense of others, it is unethical. These types of behaviors can't be defined in a set of rules. If a set of rules worked, we would be living in a moral paradise because we have plenty of written rules. Naming a dozen behaviors that preserve the integrity of our professions may be useful in the work world but result in huge gaps in what we should be doing on a daily basis.

You won't find a single professional "code of ethics" that addresses life's behaviors in general. None of them guides us to behaviors where we let a person into our lane during rush hour, greet our office workers with a smile, remember someone's birthday, or provide a hug for a grieving friend. But these behaviors are second nature to those who live by ethics, those who are guided by living their lives for the good of others.

It's possible never to have been caught in an ethical violation in one's life and still be the most insensitive jerk on earth. Plenty of these jerks are among us—they operate without a heart and within the rules. No one is calling them to task on their behaviors, and they never get caught. I've even worked with people who have memorized a code of ethics and can spout it out at will and talk about it in college courses. Yet, turn around, and they are gossiping and attempting to run down someone's reputation or life. They do this because they are the most insecure people among us. Their tool for remaining afloat in their dog-eat-dog philosophy includes "hurting others if I see them as a threat." Their happiness depends on their perceived position of power among others, instead of taking joy in promoting good will toward others.

The only true solution to any problem is the solution where all parties involved gain something. An adult is capable of spanking a child, punishing, and exercising control over him or her, but in doing so, no solution is taught. It's not unlike the gossiping adults who spread ill will because they are focused on their personal insecurity rather than a mutual solution. Certainly, the exercise of "getting all of that anger out of my body" was performed, but it didn't provide a template for how to work together toward a common solution in the future. Abusing power generates resentment. If people believe that they can solve a problem by abusing others (whether the abuse be physical, psychological, or emotional), they have in fact solved nothing at all, and they are actually creating new problems.

For those same reasons, we can snap at the clerk at the counter, but all it will get us in return is poorer service and an angrier world. The same holds true for how we treat co-workers, our family members, or any other person we interact with. Aggression creates new problems—it doesn't solve them.

So often we are quick to think of why our needs are not being met, and we miss others around us whose needs are greater than ours. Not long ago I was standing in line at a local supermarket in the express line, waiting to check out (we all know these situations where Murphy's Laws are in full force—whichever line we choose will surely be the slowest). In this case, my line was the slowest in the store, and the poor clerk was not having a banner performance. The line was held up for at least three customers in a row as the young girl struggled with a wrong price on the frozen peas, the wrong weight of the bananas, the wrong change, and now she couldn't get the credit card machine to work. The customers weren't happy, and most were either grumbling under their breaths or out loud. The manager was short on patience as he finally helped her to get the credit card machine to work. He then apologized in a curt voice, "I'm afraid that this is Suzie's first day, and it seems like there are a few things that she's not paying attention to."

Suzie stood about 5'2" and all of ninety pounds in her freshly laundered clerk's shirt and a brand new badge with her name on it. She looked to be about seventeen years old and did her best to take the feedback, but it was clear that it was getting to her as her eyes filled with tears.

I had now moved up to second place in the line. There was only one person in front of me, and she looked to be about eighty years old and about four feet ten inches tall. She carefully set her pocketbook on the counter next to a couple of items then looked up to make eye contact with Suzie. She then reached across the counter and gently placed a hand on Suzie's. In a soft voice she said, "You know what I think honey? I think you're doing a good job."

The young woman forced a smile and took a deep breath. I noticed tears forming in the corners of her eyes. Suzie sniffed and began to wipe the tears away with the back of her hands. She then swallowed a big gulp and said, "Thank you..." Her voice quivered as she swallowed again and said, "...you just made my day." Through her tears she then offered a bright smile back to the elderly woman.

It occurred to me that this tiny woman used a grand total of five seconds and a few words to make another person's day. Years from now Suzie will probably remember her job (like most of us do remember our first minimum wage job), and she may remember the angry customers, but more than likely she will remember the kind woman who made her day.

In some ways that woman made my day too. I remember being frustrated as I waited like all the other customers. But instead of responding to her frustration, this woman chose to see another's suffering and responded to it. In the end it had a tremendous effect on another human being.

It occurred to me that the rest of us were standing in line thinking of how the situation could change to make "us" happier. The elderly woman was thinking, "There is someone in pain, how can I make her happier?"

When we think of all of the people in the world who believe they are loving persons, it seems that there are fewer who actually live their philosophy in every moment. Imagine following this woman around for a day. She is a powerful force and making an amazing difference in the world! All four feet ten inches of her.

Strong people offer solutions; miserable people offer complaints. "This line should move faster! I shouldn't have to wait so long! What kind of a business do you run here?!"

The only true solutions are those that strengthen our relationships. It was easy to ruin the young girl's day, but all it served was a temporary gratification of one person's needs. It did nothing to help the problem. The poor girl in the story needed help, patience, and understanding. She wasn't about to become a better employee if she was continually hurting throughout her day.

It's impossible to foster resilience with cruelty. When we think of the above situation, we have to remember all of those times in our lives where someone was belittled or hurt, and it wasn't a life-threatening event. Our overreactions to minor events are having a cumulative effect on the world. Think of a job you had where every task was treated like it was a war zone. When people are snapping at you, treating you like an object, and stomping on your dignity, how do you feel? Now transfer that to a classroom or a family and imagine how the child feels when we are doing these things to him or her. Does a dropped plate of spaghetti result in twenty lashings? As adults, we've dropped our plates and spilled our milk (not as often as our children—because we are experienced and more coordinated), but when it happens do we expect the whole family to give us a series of tongue lashings? No, we would like a little understanding, and a little help cleaning up—just like the child.

If you've ever lost your connection to a boss, or felt less than motivated on a job where people are mean, then you will realize how children become complacent, angry, and resentful when they are in similar situations. Unfortunately, these acts are creating the blueprints for a dysfunctional child. The child is not choosing to be dysfunctional—ongoing acts of cruelty are creating resentment. Patience begets patience, kindness begets kindness, and anger begets anger.

A major mistake we make in creating our own resilience and resilience in children is the myth that we can promote fairness

> ## Son, I agree. Life's not fair. Get used to it and get back to work.
>
> ## Dad

by inflicting pain. "It's not fair! You made me wait in line so you deserve my shopper's wrath!"

When we consider the possible outcomes every time we are hostile toward others, the thing that seems sure is that hostility does little to create kindness. Is hostility what we really desire? Is this the best fairness? Do we want to move humankind toward a world of vindication?

Miserable people are convinced that life has not been fair to them. Their thinking is flawed in that they confuse "inconveniences" with "fairness." Having to wait in line, paying taxes, having to return deficient store items, and getting stuck in traffic jams are all inconveniences. The miserable person, however, will spend the entire day consumed with the perception regarding how "these things always happen to me!" The miserable tend to be on eternal missions of lashing out at the world which they see as inherently unfair to them.

Resilient people tend to avoid hostile attitudes because they see inconveniences for just what they are—a given in life. They learn to deal with them.

Resilient people tend to teach children that life will more often be a roller coaster than a perfectly tuned piano. As a result, children understand that life is better enjoyed when we (the adults) realize that long lines are necessary if one wants to get through the line. We can certainly grow our own apples, but personally I prefer to have someone else grow them, and then stand in line to buy them.

If the frustrated girl in the previous story had her way, she would have had a perfectly flawless day. No one in this world wanted the line to move quicker than she. The only good outcome for this frustrating event was her encounter with a person who was willing to use five seconds to be empathic, kind, and positive.

One can be a pressure cooker with brains boiling because life doesn't live up to a perfect outcome, or one can think about bright, positive outcomes. What makes the world a better place? Sarcasm, anger, cruelty? Or, optimism and a soft pat of the hand?

One-Minute Reflection: Compassion

For the following items, place a check next to those that apply to you (even if they are only partially true). Check any that have applied to you in the past year.

___At times, getting ahead has to be more important than my loved ones. Besides, they already know I love them.

___If I had to choose between having 20 extra hours a week with my loved ones, or 200 extra dollars to spend on them, I would choose the money most of the time.

___I realize that I snap at some people, but you have to be a little aggressive to make it in this world.

___I'm nice mostly to the people who are close to me; outside of them, it's not as important to be nice to others in public. Most of them won't see me again anyway.

___When I'm upset with people, it's easier for me to drop a few sarcastic remarks than to ask for what I want. Besides, a few well-intended sarcastic hints will often get people moving.

___I believe that because I survived my parent's spankings and toughness, then my kids can do the same.

Continue with the chapter; we will revisit these items at the end.

MENTAL SKILL #4—CONTROL
Resilient people exercise personal control.

> **When we lose our patience, it's like putting on a blindfold and swinging a baseball bat without caring whom it hits.**

Healthy adults and children see life as welcoming rather than threatening. In doing so, they make themselves patient and approachable, rather than threatening and paranoid. The essential key to personal control is to have the ability constantly to separate real problems from imagined ones. What are real problems? Getting stuck in traffic? Waiting too long in a line? Who left the cap off the toothpaste?

We needlessly create a world where these issues dominate our lives. To have a child in a diabetic coma is a real problem. To have a child with intractable epileptic seizures is a real problem. Having inoperable cancerous tumors is a real problem. To have a loved one struck down by a drunken driver is a real problem.

We waste precious time in our lives losing personal control as we scream about poor restaurant service, socks on the floor, and children having to take too many bathroom breaks on our vacations.

These are inconveniences; they are not problems. To build resilience in ourselves and our children, we need to model a healthy objective view on what's important in life. We need to sort our real problems versus imagined ones. When we have an abundance of imagined problems, we lose our personal control. We lose our impulse control, and we lash out at things that are meaningless in the large scale of life. The result is an abnormal range of behaviors, emotions, and moods.

Not long ago I stood in front of two men at an airport who went on a non-stop rant of complaints as we waited in line. The line went for some distance, and every few minutes, about five people were allowed to go up an escalator to the metal detectors. The two men incessantly spouted a series of complaints, "They should have more lines...more staff... Why aren't they more organized? What the hell's wrong with these people? I can't believe these idiots!"

The only thing that any of us knew for sure was that we were all destined to wait in this line for at least thirty minutes. In front of me in the line were two women who looked to be in their late forties. They began joking about the line and escalator. In short time they were laughing out loud at the things they were saying, "This must be a great escalator if we have to wait so long! I'll bet it's a Disney escalator! I'll bet that some of these people camped out just to ride on this thing!" The more they joked, the more they laughed. Soon they were wiping away tears and holding their stomachs. "I'll bet that Goofy is at the top! Look there's two more people who get to go! Lucky them! Only four more people until the magic escalator ride!"

As I listened to them, I couldn't help but laugh as well; it was great comic relief for a relatively common inconvenience. The crowning glory was watching the two women when they finally got to go up the escalator. For the entire twenty-second trip, they held their hands over their heads, squealing "Wheee!" as though they were riding a roller coaster, and laughing hysterically the whole way to the top. Many of the people in the airport looked at them as though they were crazy; I thought they were hysterical.

The lesson is simple: an inconvenience can be turned into misery or a roller coaster ride. Being able to enjoy life's little inconvenient moments is the glue that holds our sanity together, and the glue is located in our heads.

In everything we do, we are creating memories. When we search our past for the most enjoyable moments in our lives, we often find a similarity in them, quite often they involved a time when we were hysterical over something that struck us as incredibly funny. I believe these women will probably remember their silly moment for a long time to come. "Remember when we were stuck in the airport...."

At the other end of the spectrum, we have two men who were only feeding their hostility toward the world. Their time in line was the same as it was for the rest of us, and it did no good only to see misery. They too will have a string of memories and say, "Remember when we were stuck in the airport..."

One of best things we can do in modeling behavior as a parent, teacher, and leader of others is to exhibit a healthy normal range of reactions to life's events. If others look to us for guidance and leadership, we can only expect them to have what we have. If we have an abnormal range of behaviors, emotions, and moods, we can expect no different from them. In the examination of our own reactions, do we have normal anxiety toward the issues and challenges in our own lives? Or, are we jittery, reactive, obsessive, and/or paranoid? Can we go with the flow of the minor neurotics in our offices and daily interactions? Or, do we have to put them all in their place? Control them? Show them who's right? Show them who's boss? Gossip about them? All of these reactions are a loss of energy and an inefficient way to approach life. We have to determine how we want to spend our time on earth and determine how we want to teach our children to spend their time on earth.

We should expect anxiety and mood change in our lives, but we need to recognize that there is a choice in regard to effective and ineffective approaches. Are we choosing to take life's small inconveniences and turn them into tantrum-laced tirades? If our child is running five minutes late for the bus, are we turning it into a major crisis? In the final analysis, children will never remember what it was that they were late for, but it's a guarantee that they will begin to resent the verbal abuse. Ultimately this is how they will remember their parents and teachers. It also applies to our everyday lives. We all know that co-worker who goes to DEFCON ONE every time the copier is broken, or explodes every time his or her computer goes down.

If we as adults act out in this manner, we shouldn't be surprised when our children are slamming their toy chests, stomping their feet, and losing control when they've misplaced their dolls. When we have the choice to save our children from our own neurotic patterns, it only makes sense that we focus on these changes in ourselves. Imagine years from now that a child is experiencing poor relationships, a lack of patience, sleepless nights, and psychological anguish. Now imagine that we have choices today that can save him from these things. Saving ourselves from our own neurotic patterns not only saves us, it saves our children. This could be the most wonderful gift we can give to them.

One-Minute Reflection: Control

For the following items, place a check next to those that apply to you (even if they are only partially true). Check any that have applied to you in the past year.

___My happiness today will depend on how others are treating me.

___I have been known to pitch a fit or two, mostly when I'm standing up for my rights.

___I tend to lose patience mostly with the pace of life—slow lines, people, traffic, etc.

___When a person does a stupid thing (in traffic, at work, in public, etc.), I get upset, and it can sometimes ruin a good portion of my day.

___I speak my mind quite often, but I think that people need to get tougher rather than my getting softer.

___A good old-fashioned tongue-lashing and ass-chewing never did anyone any harm; besides it made me tougher.

Continue with the chapter; we will revisit these items at the end.

MENTAL SKILL #5—OPTIMISM
Resilient people see life for its possibilities.

> **Most people would rather be certain they're miserable than risk being happy.**
>
> **Robert Anthony**

Among human beings, there is a range of optimism. Most of us know someone who is extraordinarily optimistic. We enjoy her company because spending time in her presence provides us with encouragement. We also know the pessimists, and conversely, all they can offer the world is discouragement.

Optimistic people stay in the positive lane of life because they do not see distress as a curse, but rather as a given in life. Optimism is perhaps the most valuable of all resilience skills in conquering distress. Research shows that optimists live longer, have fewer health problems, more meaningful relationships, and are overall better problem solvers. They tend to be more productive because they not only encourage others; they also have the ability to be "self-encouraging."

If we were to poll parents, teachers, and leaders, and ask them, what would you like for your loved ones? it would be hard to imagine that they would say, "I hope they live a stress-filled, short life! I want them to have numerous health problems, miserable marriages and families, ***and*** most of all I want them be in psychological anguish when they solve their problems!" This statement is absurd, but it seems that's what we want for our loved ones if this is all that we can give them!

Optimists are constantly a target for hostile people, mostly because the negative person is convinced that life is better lived in crisis rather than adventure. Most people would much rather be around an optimist because they can take every minor crisis and have fun with it.

Several years ago I was in a car bounding down a dirt road when the front tire blew out. My friend pulled the car over and jumped out to look at the damage. The first words out of his mouth were, "Hey! Aren't you glad that didn't happen on the highway?"

I laughed because we were stuck in the woods with a car full of kids, and the first thing that he thought of was *not* "Oh poor me...Oh why the hell does this happen to me?" Rather, his thoughts were positive. It is one of the reasons that my friend Dale is one of the special people in my life. He's a college administrator, and people gravitate toward him. His staff wants to work for him, he has friends in abundance, and his popularity has no bounds. It is all for one simple reason—optimism. People love to be around him. He sees adventures and challenges where others see doom and gloom.

Dale and I took off the flat tire and lined up five kids for a hike down the mountain. He clapped his hands together and hollered to the kids, "Hey guys! How much luckier could we be? We get to go back down to town *and* do you know what we forgot to get the last time we were there? Ice cream!" The kids all cheered. I did too. If there was anyone in this world who I could choose to have with me in a flat-tire situation, he would be Dale.

The hike was long, but the kids made a game of who got to roll the old tire. When we got to the service station, Dale struck up a conversation with the old mechanic and chatted like they were old friends. The mechanic didn't have the new tire we needed but spent the next twenty minutes fishing through a pile of old tires until he found his best "balding" tire that would enable us to make it through our trip. In the end it cost a whopping five dollars. We all got ice cream bars, and the kids skipped alongside the tire as we rolled it back to the car.

When we got back to camp, Dale's wife came up to the car and before she could ask what took us so long, he jumped out of the car and pointed to the wheel, "Honey, have you ever seen a better looking five dollar tire in your life?"

Minor crises and how we handle them tend to affect everyone's emotions. I realized how easy it would have been to turn the day into chaos instead of an adventure. If we all lost our patience, screamed, kicked the car, complained to the mechanic, and hollered at the children—what effect would it have? Would it make the day go quicker? Would it get us there faster? Would we spend less money? Would life be better?

The only thing that could have happened with negativity was that our lives would have been less than they were before. Our relationships would have become more distant, and we would remember the day not as one of joy, but one of anguish. And here's the biggest question—how would our kids remember their dads?

People in our lives who are like Dale often turn out to be some of the greatest teachers we know, and it's all done informally. Optimists maintain the same outlook at the supermarket as they do on the job. In the case of my friend, he treats the custodian the same as he treats his wife and children—with dignity and respect. That's the reason why people will be more than willing to work hard for him, help him, and give their time to him. Positive people are simply attractive people, and we go out of our way to help them.

It is a unique talent to take any setback and immediately envision a positive outcome. One of the reasons why optimism is such an important skill to teach is because it is simply the art of effective problem solving. It also is the cornerstone of self-appreciation. Angry people are not only ineffective problem solvers—they tend to be self-hating.

All of us have our moments when we are less than proud of how we reacted to a situation, but we have to remember that distress is nothing more than an unsolved problem in our minds. Some problems *should* take longer and require more emotion and energy. When we grieve, lose relationships we are strongly attached to, or have a strong investment in a life or the health of someone close to us, we naturally should be more troubled than issues such as, "who spilled the orange juice at the dinner table." The key is to ask ourselves—Am I investing ten gallons of adrenaline into a one-pint problem? So, how do we teach kids to put a pint of adrenaline into a one-pint problem? Clearly, there is only one way to teach it, and this is to live it.

The blown tire above was clearly a one-pint problem, and when optimistically considered it was fun for everyone. If we are too closely attached to the ideas that "Nothing must go wrong today! And, I must get back to the camp in perfect timely order!"—the result will be obvious tension and distress. Optimists are not too closely attached to perfect order, which is why they are so much more effective in challenging times. When we think about our everyday lives, it's important to remind ourselves that our children are learning to respond to the world in the same way that we respond to the spilled cereal, the messy room, or the forgetfulness that they had today.

Consequently, we should not become too attached to such ideas as "I must never be late for work or it's the end of the world! No one must disagree with me in the meeting—or it's the end of our relationship! No one must make mistakes! Nothing must go wrong today!" Pessimistic adults are always teaching. They are teaching intolerance and hostility. Optimistic adults are also teaching in all that they do. They are teaching kindness and understanding. They are teaching resilience.

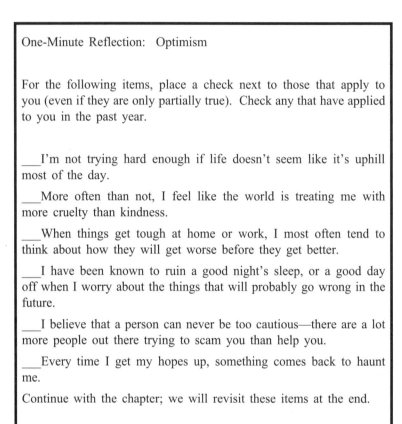

One-Minute Reflection: Optimism

For the following items, place a check next to those that apply to you (even if they are only partially true). Check any that have applied to you in the past year.

___I'm not trying hard enough if life doesn't seem like it's uphill most of the day.

___More often than not, I feel like the world is treating me with more cruelty than kindness.

___When things get tough at home or work, I most often tend to think about how they will get worse before they get better.

___I have been known to ruin a good night's sleep, or a good day off when I worry about the things that will probably go wrong in the future.

___I believe that a person can never be too cautious—there are a lot more people out there trying to scam you than help you.

___Every time I get my hopes up, something comes back to haunt me.

Continue with the chapter; we will revisit these items at the end.

Becoming Resilient—the complete package

Every time we pick up the paper and read about a school shooting or a murder in our community, it causes most of us to have our hearts drop. Strong, resilient people don't have the need to use violence to express their anger. We don't read about the suicides as often as murders. For children, there are four times as many victims from suicide as there are from homicide. When children are unable to overcome life's obstacles they give up on life—they don't understand the sacredness of others' lives or their own. They don't have the tools to bounce back. In either case, we are losing precious lives and precious human potential. To give them the resilience they need and deserve has to become a central focus of our approach to life. Not all of life is rosy, but learning to deal with the difficult times results in a gift to others—the gift of joy.

One-Minute Reflection: The Complete Package

Go back and add up all of those items you checked as currently applying to you or have applied to you in the past year.

Score of 21 to 30
You are very discontented with life and your personal relationships. At least you were honest and you realize that you need some work. Sooner or later, if things don't change, you will hit a brick wall either in your relationships or in your own nervous breakdown. It takes a lot of energy to survive life in this much anguish. For the most part you know that you are doing it to yourself, but often blame the world for the lack of joy in your life.

Score of 11 to 20
You oscillate between good days and bad days. Sometimes you are eaten up by your own guilt. Things slip out of your mouth and then you regret them later. You are easily swayed to the dark side when you hang around with pessimistic or gossipy people. You have to make a conscious decision as to how much you will be infected by the bad attitudes in the world.

Score of 1 to 10
You're enjoying life but not as much as you would like to. You probably count your blessings, but also realize that you would like to count them a little more often. You would like to tell people around you a little more often how much they mean to you. You would also like to let your head hit the pillow every night and feel more thankful for the good things and the good people around you.

Score of 0
You're either perfect, and you need to be bronzed, or you're lying and you need to proceed directly to counseling. We all struggle with becoming the resilient person we would like to be, and we all have faults. We all live with a little guilt and a little anxiety as we balance our goals, relationships, and desires. When we are in our self-pity moments, we can fall into the traps of not feeling contented, or we give up, don't care, snap at people, or see the gloom instead of the bright side of life.

For all readers:
Go back and look at each of the areas and decide which one needs the most work and decide which one may have the most potential for making your loved ones miserable. Do you need to be more content with what you have? Do you need to be more open to changes and growth? Do you need to put your loved ones ahead of your tempers? Do you need to see the brighter side of life and believe in the goodness of life?

Begin to make a journal and decide what changes are the most important. In order to become more resilient, you not only need to add things, you need to let go of some things. Money, power, and privileges are not at stake when we talk about resilience. The only things that are at stake are our relationships and our personal joy in life. We all have to give ourselves the gift of resilience before we are able to give it to our children

If we want to be better people for our friends, loved ones, and children, we have to decide what we are willing to do to make *ourselves* strong, and in doing so, we are giving the greatest gift that we can ever create—we are giving them *us*.

"Toughness" is not something to be beaten into children. "Toughness" is an accumulation of positive resources. It's never too late in life to develop these resources, and the best way to give these resources is to own them. The greatest benefits, however, are more smiles, more laughter, and more love.

From Innocent Children to World Leaders—Collaboration provides the foundation for a Peaceful Coexistence

Jennifer's face grew red. She clenched her left hand into a fist and pointed at me with her right hand as she ranted non-stop for at least five minutes. Jennifer was a thirty-two year-old mother who had come to me for counseling because of her on-going problem with alcohol, but the alcohol wasn't the issue that was upsetting her. It all started with one question in regard to her five-year-old son, "Have you ever hit Peter in anger?"

The secretaries in the outer office reported that they could hear every word she screamed, "I know what the f #^* you people are up to! Who the hell do you think you are?! You've got no f *^#ing right to tell me how to treat my child! It's my child; don't tell me what to do with my kid!"

Prior to this meeting, I had the opportunity to spend some time with Peter in the waiting room before some of the sessions with his mother. He was lively and interacted like a lot of other five year olds until his mother was present. He reminded me of a turtle that would pull his head into his shell. He was always on guard, jumpy, and looked like he was on the verge of a nervous breakdown, and all this occurred within a few seconds of his mother's arrival. It prompted me to ask the question that set her off. The sad reality is in the mother's perception he was "her child" to do with as she pleased. She never spoke of Peter as a human being and only referred to him as "the kid," as she would throw a condescending nod in his direction.

123

After the meeting, she was shaking him in the hallway when I did my best to intervene and gently suggest that her behaviors were unnecessary. Her response was, "It's my child; don't tell me what to do with my kid!" The only thing for us to do was to contact the Department of Social Services.

During the years in my line of work, I have come to realize that one of the biggest misconceptions people have in relationships is the myth of ownership. It boils down to this—no single human being owns another human being. What many parents don't understand is that they don't own their children. When a child is born, he or she is a citizen of the state, not a possession of the parent. It is the duty of any civilized society to protect its citizens. The parent has no right to abuse the child, but unfortunately many believe they do have that right. We've seen videotapes of parents caught on camera as they slap, hit, or shake their children. They honestly believe that the child is their property to do with as they please.

The same mentality holds true in many other relationships. When I was in college, I witnessed a man hitting a woman in a parking lot. When another man tried to intervene, the abusive man said, "It's none of your damn business—she's *my* wife." It was as though he thought he had some precedence for violating another human being.

No one owns another human being, and it's especially important for us to realize this in the case of defenseless children. We have enormous responsibility to care for them, but that doesn't give us the right to abuse them. It is a crime. One of these days I may end up getting attacked because of my strong beliefs. As I have grown older and as my two boys have grown up, I find myself getting a little bolder in public and trying to ask parents in a soft voice not to hit their children. I hear parents saying, "Mind your own damn business, it's *my* kid!"

This *right to violence* mentality is very common, and it is continuing the chain of violence into the next generation. A friend of mine is principal of a middle school. She described a parent who came in to the school on the first day and said, "I just want to let you know that I told my son, if anyone messes with him, he has my permission to hit them." The principal replied, "Then we also have to let you know that there will be consequences for that type of behavior." The parent retorted, "Then I will have to let you know that I will fight you every step of the way." This is a typical case of people who want it both ways—they want a society to be lawful, but believe they have the right to take the law into their own hands. This is not the old west, and condoning violence on a playground will have long-term effects in breaking down our social structures.

I think about the people I have worked with after counseling ends. I think about Peter all the time, and I wonder what happened to him. He was a sweet kid when he came out of his shell. He made me realize how much we need to work with, and educate, parents. He made me realize how easy it is to take away the strength of a child.

The weakest people among us are those who have the greatest desire to exercise control over others. This especially holds true for neurotic, controlling parents and adults. Their children turn out to have relationships as weak as theirs. The strongest parents I've ever met are those who are constantly building relationships, collaborating, creating mutual goals, and nurturing the strength in their children—not taking it away. Consequently, these strong parents produce the most well-adjusted children I've ever worked with. With every interaction that empowers their child, they are building hope.

Hope is the product of collaborative relationships. If we look at human history, the most powerful people have been those who provided hope through empowering people, not controlling them.

Martin Luther King, Gandhi, and Mother Theresa are not mentioned in our history books when we talk of power, because we mistakenly define power as *controlling* others. In our own time, we need to realize that the most powerful people in our country are not those who wield political or fiscal power, but the Oprah Winfreys, Jimmy Carters, and Nelson Mandelas who have empowered people to take a stand for something, chase their dreams, reach for their potential, and do things for others.

> **If you think you are leading and turn around to see no one following, then you are just taking a walk.**
>
> **Benjamin Hooks**

The only thing that can happen with exercising power over people is an oppressive relationship where personal strength is robbed from one person to the benefit of another. When human beings are subjected to relationships where they are oppressed, they gravitate toward one of two options. They either think of rebelling or obeying. In the case of rebellion, it's because they believe that fighting back may offer them new freedom and perhaps offer them the upper hand in the power struggle. In the case of obeying, one has given up hope.

In both cases the oppression results in a struggle for power. All of our relationships could be classified as either having a power balance or imbalance. Most of us can think of the harsh dominant boss, or someone's abusive spouse, or the cruel parent who constantly uses excessive force with his or her child. These people have lost their ability to control the relationship through collaboration. They pursue and exercise force, believing it is the only way to have their needs met.

Most of us have been victimized at one time or another by someone's need for control. The result was a situation where we were demoralized, broken, or exploited. We can also relate to the psychological processes we endured: depression, anxiety, and loss of joy in living. Exercising power and seeking to gain position, advantage, and control of others may be the one of the greatest crimes we witness. In some countries where women are victims of oppression and considered second-class citizens, it's been estimated that up to 70% of the female population have enough symptoms to be classified as clinically depressed.

We are social creatures who thrive on cooperative efforts. If we look around us to our houses, cars, computers, roads, and buildings, we will see the evidence of enormous cooperative efforts. Any one of us individually could try to build a house, or construct a car, or devise a computer, but chances are none of us could independently create all of the things that we enjoy. Individual rights and collaborative relationships are essential in all human productivity. It doesn't matter whether it is a relationship of two, a family, team, culture or society. The principle remains the same—when we work together, we have less distress and destruction. When we limit individual rights, we become psychopathological and see the worst side of humans.

The ability to collaborate is a skill of vital importance for creating peace within our relationships, reducing our tension, and adding productivity to our daily interactions. This chapter will look at the five universal characteristics of a strong collaborative relationship. They are the same regardless of age, gender, status, or position. First, we need to **Create "Real" Quality Time**. In order to make the biggest difference in any relationship, it has to have true quality as well as quantity. We must redefine the meaning of "quality time." Just because we are spending time with someone, it doesn't mean we are building the relationship, or the individual.

We also need to **Change from Debating to Relating.** Much of our communication with others doesn't focus on mutual outcomes but rather emphasizes "who will win the battle." We can't even begin to relate until we drop our battle axes.

Another important aspect of a collaborative relationship is dependency. With the emphasis on independence in our culture, we often lose sight of the value of our cooperation. If we **Build Healthy Dependency** into our relationships, we learn to depend on others without taking advantage of them. In order to nourish those relationships, we need to develop an awareness of *how* we communicate and how we sever the connections we already have. Mutual dependency can only grow stronger if we can **Emphasize Truthful Communication.** Learning to say what we want in a constructive manner is the quickest route to stress reduction and mutual respect.

Finally, we need to develop a healthy view of learning principles. It's important to **Create Consequences not Punishment** when we are trying to guide others toward appropriate behaviors. Earlier in the book I mentioned that we need to drop our egos. In learning to collaborate, we need to prize *harmony* as a central philosophy in our values. The ability to be a strong collaborator is not just a goal but a lifelong practice. If our desires in life must be met at the expense of others, then we are missing out on the meaning and purpose of life itself.

> **Smile at each other; smile at your spouse; smile at your children—it doesn't matter who it is—and that will help you grow in greater love for each person**
>
> **Mother Teresa**

"I really think that it's the quality of time that's important in my children's life, not the quantity," said Mary. She reached for another tissue and blew her nose. She was a thirty-five year old mother who came to counseling because she felt her family was falling apart. Her comment about the "quality" and "quantity" of time with her children is common—common and sad. Her tears, sadness, anxiety, and frustration were all testimony to her mental state.

Mary is not unlike many other parents who use a lot of energy defending how they spend their time with their children. Not unlike our culture, she was in search of a quick fix—a two-minute recipe to re-connect with her children. She wanted to fix things and fix them now. Mary was fighting with her teenage son, her nine year-old daughter, and her husband. She wanted a couple of counseling sessions to tell her how to repair it, and she cried throughout each of them. Mary's family was falling apart, but neither she nor her husband was willing to alter how they distributed their time. She described her half-hour of daily "quality" time as driving her kids to soccer practices, driving through fast food restaurants, asking them if they got their homework done, and telling them to clean their rooms.

We see a lot of parents like Mary who have hearts of gold. They love their children, want good things for them, and yet find

129

themselves frustrated by the tension in their relationships. In order to get a firm grasp on what is happening in our culture, we have to stop and pay attention to our values, our needs, and whether in fact our lives reflect what we say is important.

The best place to start is in examining our daily lives. We spend a lot of time with people during the course of the day, and not all time is the same. When we prize the relationship, we fashion that time to be effective. Think about the last time you worked with a boss or a co-worker who had little interest in your well-being. Chances are, he treated you as an object, and you resented it. We have to realize that we have the capability of dehumanizing our children with these same tactics. All we have to do is look at what most of us seek in our personal relationships. We don't look for friends and partners by saying, "Gee, I think I would really like to have a friend who abuses me and keeps me in my place." If we think about what *we* want in relationships, we have to do our best to give our children the same.

The only way to have a friend is to be one.

Ralph Waldo Emerson

How we spend time with others will determine the respect, closeness, and trust between us. It isn't about quality *or* quantity; it's about both. We need a lot of time, and we need to make as much quality time as possible. Not all time is equal because our time with others may take on a different purpose depending on what we are trying to accomplish. If it's cleaning time in your home and one person is scrubbing the toilet while the other is vacuuming, we are working together toward a goal but not necessarily creating a closer bond. There are a lot of relationships in this world that are functional but have little relational quality.

I read an interview with a distraught mother who described her family as a "well-run ship." Everyone got off to school on time, everyone had jobs around the house, there was food on the table, a clean house, professional parents, and money in the bank. The perfect American family? It looked that way except that they had to rush to the hospital a few days earlier to have stitches put in their daughter's wrists after her suicide attempt.

If all of our time is spent gaining ground in the day to day tasks but denying each other, we are missing out on the only thing that really matters in life—each other. It's possible to produce a life of numerous physical comforts but deny the emotional ones. In all relationships, the emotional needs are the ones that are the most important, and we need to nurture them with quality time. In order to understand quality time, we also need to realize that a lot of time is productive, but can't count as quality. There are four different forms of relational time, and each one has a different purpose. We have supervised time, guidance time, productive time, and quality time.

Supervised time is when we have an authority present. We are available but with distance. It's like on your job. Someone is available but not breathing down your neck. He is there when you need him; he makes you feel secure but not oppressed. With children, it could be analogous to the "Kool-Aid" house where the whole neighborhood can hang out, play, and do their own thing within certain appropriate boundaries. We always know that there is someone to bandage a knee or help with a dispute.

Guidance time is helping with expertise. Teaching, help with homework, coaching, cooking, building, showing our six-year-old the fine points of scrubbing a pan or instructing an eight-year-old on how to start a load of laundry, are examples of guidance time.

Productive time is when we all have certain jobs, areas of strength, and missions, but not necessarily together. We all work for the common good but may not cross paths. Productive time is usually mutually agreed upon, "I will trim the hedges while you cut the lawn."

We need all of these types of time for any productive relationship, and all of them may have aspects that may have quality, but none of them is spent for the sole purpose of quality. Quality time is face-to-face interaction about things that do matter and don't matter. This does not include the driving of the kids to the soccer practice, or the drive-through at the fast food restaurant, or the questions of, "Did you get your homework done... feed the cat...pick up your room..." Quality time is precisely what it says. First, it is **quality**—meaning we talk about the real events in our lives, the issues that are bothering us, the things that are fun, and things that we are interested in. I learned my lesson with my own teens when I stopped asking, "How was your day?" The only response I could generate was the generic shoulder shrug with the "I dunno" answer. We changed our strategies at the dinner table and started asking such questions as—"who was the most obnoxious person you ran into today?" Now, you get a totally different response. They became animated, vocal, and full of life as they described their math teacher, or a kid on their team. It also allowed our kids to see the real side of their parents as we talked about obnoxious or interesting things in our day too. We also would ask questions like, "What was the high and low point of your day?"

The second part of "quality time" is **time** not moments. It literally means hours, not minutes. It means planning as many weekly meals as possible, putting down the TV controller, and sometimes putting aside our own hobbies. If the activity is spent with both individuals looking in the same direction (at the TV, through the windshield, or at a movie screen), then we are not looking at each other. If the result of our rushed, high-earning society is a culture of little quality time, then our priorities are bent out of shape. It also means that the average child's well-being and character in an American family are not priorities in their parent's lives.

Quality time also serves children to learn the art of relating. If we are playing a board game, discussing the day's events, or talking about one's dreams, we are exercising a number of relational skills that we don't get from any of the other forms of time. We are listening, paying respect, dedicating time to their emotional well-being, devoting time to our mutual interests, and investing in our present and future joy.

The most ridiculous thing we can ever do is make excuses or rationalize why we *don't* have the ability to spend time with our loved one. We need time, and we need to make time. How much extra time would we have if the television was turned off on school nights? If meals were planned instead of "catching them on the fly?" If Sundays were arranged so that time could be spent planning out the week so all kids take turns cooking, cleaning, and doing their own laundry, [Believe me, any elementary-school-age child can learn to make a salad, fold socks, and clean a toilet—and by middle school they should be able to do these things independently. This is something I will talk about this more in the next section—Collaborative Relating.]

Supervised, guidance, productive, and quality time are all important, and all have their own purpose. Supervised time allows us to protect our children—they don't need to be running wild, accessing all things on the internet, and watching all the shows on cable TV. Our job is to protect them from the variety of things in this world which they are too young to make educated decisions about.

Guidance time allows us to develop strong independent life skills. We may be helping others in things we've already learned —such as house chores, school tasks, and personal care. In the long run we want them to be able to leave home with the ability to cook an egg, scrub a bathtub, or wax a floor. We create a tremendous disservice to them by not holding them accountable for their own life-skills.

Productive time is essential in any relationship. If all members are contributing to the nuts and bolts of the operation, then we all prosper. Now, having looked at all of the above, we can also reflect on the "well run" family with the suicidal daughter. There is a possibility that she may have a serious chronic depressive condition, but in most cases like these, the child is crying out for a connection to anyone who will care. What we hear in suicide notes is, "...no one to talk to...feeling all alone...no one cares..." It isn't enough to tell our children, "You can come to me for anything." We have to create a presence *before* the attempt—not after. If a child from a "well run" house is slashing her wrists, there is a strong possibility that there is no healthy connection in the home.

We don't grow closer to others simply because they are physically present. If this were the case, a houseplant would be more useful than a human; at least it is always there! Being emotionally present isn't just an episodic appearance, it's a sense of attachment that is founded upon the mutual emotional reliance that *this person really does care about me...this person will not judge me regardless of what I bring to her...this person will not condemn me for my faults and will not make me feel like a lesser human being if he hears of my pain...this person will stick with me through thick and thin...this person would never do anything purposefully to hurt me...I can and will always be able trust this person.*

However quality time is apportioned, it will be about our personal investment in having fun together, having tears together, and having concerns together. It may be over dinner, it may be your teen plopping himself on the foot of your bed and telling you about his day, it may be the mutual enjoyment of your eight-year-old daughter telling you about her science-fair project, or it may be your spouse needing you for a little "venting time" at the end of the day. In all cases, the more the better, and if we are spending more time facing the TV together than facing each other, we need a major rearrangement of our time. Again, all of this goes back to placing the importance on *us* and not *me*. I may have some very important personal needs, but the nurturing of my relationships has to be evidenced in every aspect of my life.

A friend of mine works very hard as a single mother to support herself and her child. We once had a discussion about how she would love to get her doctoral degree, but she said she "could never do it" in her current situation. She had bills, a mortgage, and a number of commitments. I told her, "Sure you could, you could do it right now, but something would have to give, and you realize that the time you spend with your child at nights and the manner in which you support him is at the top of your priority list. You could get your doctorate, but your son is more important to you, and that is something you should be more proud of than any other thing in your life." I'm sure that one day she will earn her doctorate, but it may be at a time when her child is in school and in a situation where she can still afford the quality time that he deserves.

For my wife and myself, we gave up a large house and two cars to move into a basement apartment in order to finish our educations when our children were young. Several years later, we had four more college degrees between the two of us, but something had to give in order to have a lot of time with our children. We gave up a few luxuries and a good paying job. We took a risk to advance our education, but we didn't give up our time with our children. In the end, we got a slow start on our pensions, but our lifestyle improved, and it was worth it.

I remember interviewing for my doctoral program, and one of the questions that was asked in our group interview was, "What do you expect to give up in your personal life in order to get through this program?" I was the last to answer, and several of those before me said, "I expect less time with my husband...children...loved ones..." I responded by saying, "I don't expect to give up any time with my wife or my family. I will probably give up some earning power, and some sleep, but to tell you the truth, this program will be secondary to my family." After I was done with the round of interviews, I remember standing in the hallway thinking, *Damn! That was a stupid thing to say; that's probably not what they wanted to hear.* To my surprise, two other students stopped and said, "I appreciate what you said in there. It's probably not what they wanted to hear, but it was honest." Then I thought, *great, honesty will keep me out of the program.* A few moments later, Dr. Sarah Shaw, the professor who interviewed us stopped by and said, "Good answers, Steve!" Then she walked down the hallway. Five years later she hooded me at our doctoral ceremony as my kids cheered their very poor but well-educated father.

We have to decide what we are willing to give up if our children are truly at the top of our priority list. One of my friends recently turned down a higher paying job (significantly higher—he would nearly double his salary). He turned it down because it would take away several afternoons and evenings with his children each week. He told me he had a philosophy—"never trade time for money. Time with your family is the world's greatest commodity, and it pays the highest dividends."

We don't get time back when it's gone. If it's spent, it can't be re-bargained or traded back. In the end, if given the option, would we trade our finest memories in our relationships for a couple of stereos, boats, and DVD players? Some are left with cold appliances and no warm memories.

We need to do everything we can to create a healthy relationship with all the people we interact with. As adults, we can recognize the other adults in our lives whom we avoid. The reason we avoid them is simple, and it's the same reason why children avoid some adults—we want nothing to do with a no-win situation. There's a lot of pathological power out their in the form of adults who have a tremendous need to control everything in their lives. No matter how much lip service they give to an "open door," we fear them and avoid them. The people who demand the most control in life are usually the ones who feel the most "out of control" on the inside.

One-Minute Reflection: Time

For the next week, at the end of each day, take a moment to review your day. In every day we need balance. We need time for ourselves, time for life's tasks, and time for others. If you thought about how your time was spent, how would it be distributed? What percent of your day was spent with each of the following:
personal—get away time (a bath, a book, music, exercise)
mindless time (changing channels, etc.)
productive time
supervised or supervisory time
guidance time, and
quality time (or any other modes of time you've spent).

As you review your day or week, keep in mind that there isn't a perfect formula for how we should spend our time (we all need to be the judge of our own lives), but we may need to ask ourselves some of the following:

*   Am I satisfied with how I've distributed my time?
*   Did I spend time on needless things? (Guilt? Excessive worry? Obsessions)

*   Do I regret time wasted?

*   Does my time spent reflect my values?

*   Was I so consumed with saving time (rushing myself, rushing others, driving fast, losing my patience) that I actually lost time?

*   Do I defend a style of life I'm not happy with?

*   Am I willing to ask my loved ones for their time?

*   If I really want to spend my time differently, am I willing to put a lot of energy into what I really want? Or, give up?

> **If you can't find it in your heart to love others, could you, for at least one day—not hurt anyone? If each of us could do this one small thing, the world would be an infinitely better place.**
>
> **Leo Buscaglia**

Change from Debating to Relating

A few years ago I was standing in a line at a pharmacy waiting to get medication for my son's condition of epilepsy. The line was long, and it seemed like it was going to take me forever that day, but that long wait was a blessing in disguise. It forced me to stand and watch a no-holds-barred battle between a mother and her son. What I witnessed was common but shocking because it represents the direction we are headed in our culture.

The mother was in her mid-thirties and her son was about four years old. The boy threw himself on the floor, then on the candy rack, and then he threw himself on the news rack. This was occurring as he and his mother carried on a ridiculous battle of words.

"You don't love me!" he screamed.

"Well if that's true then why did I take you to a movie?" she asked in a calm voice. Each time he would scream his comment; she would use a soft voice and give her retort—as though the soft voice meant she was more mature.

"You're always mean to me!" he yelled as he flopped on the floor.

"Well if that's the case then why did I take you to get a Jolly Cheeseburger Meal? I guess you're right, I'm a mean mother, but I know someone even meaner, the little boy I brought with me!"

"I wish I had a new mother!"

"I wish I had a boy who knew how to behave!"

"I hate you. You're mean!"

"I guess I'll just have to be a mean mom and throw out all of those nice toys I bought you!"

"I want to go home!"

"That's fine. It would be a good idea if I never took you anywhere with me again!"

"I'm not waiting with you anymore!" he said as he started for the door.

The mother grabbed his arm, spun him around and said, "Oh yes you will!" The boy then proceeded to scream.

As I listened to this battle between an adult and a child, it made me think about how often we experience battles where the only goal is to win. In each of these cases, someone also has to lose. The mother and the child had the same intention—each wanted to hurt the other. While it seemed obvious to all of us standing in line that this was the most spoiled brat we had ever seen, it didn't occur to me right away that the mother was as much of a brat as the child.

Neither one of them could say what he or she wanted, but each comment was intended to bring pain to the other person. I don't blame the child, but why would a mother be motivated to cause her own child to feel pain? The only thing she wanted to do was to win this battle with her child, and in every exchange I could see their bond, and their connection to each other failing. Instead of trying to win the battle, why wasn't she trying to build the peace? Why couldn't either one of them say, "My feelings are hurt...can you help me? I'm sorry...Can we work together on this?" The child can't say it because he hasn't learned to communicate his feelings. The mother can't do it because her ego is too big—if she let herself be vulnerable, it wouldn't allow her to win her battle.

There was so much that I learned while I waited ten minutes in that line that it changed my life and some of my own relationships. I was thinking—is this me sometimes, where all I want to do is win the argument?

We teach children to fight. Sometimes these sweet calm voices that we use are still laced with hurtful intentions. This mother shouldn't wonder why she has a child who wants to hurt her feelings; it's the only strategy for meeting his needs that he has ever witnessed. After that day, I paid more attention to my interactions with my loved ones than I had ever before. I paid attention to everything I had to say to them. Is it my intention to hurt them, or build us? Is it my intention always to win control of this disagreement? Or, win the control of our relationship?

In our families, on our jobs, or in everyday interactions—how often do we hear the "Oh yes you will!" These messages can be conveyed with meanness, a soft voice, or with sarcasm—it all has the same message, "I'll show you, I'm going to come out on top in our disagreement, and I'll get there at all costs!" If the emphasis is on one person controlling the other, the connection with them is severed. It takes a lot of life to rebuild a connection from even one hurtful or sarcastic remark. We can't force a relationship to become a caring one. What will this woman say one day to her sixteen year-old when he says I don't love you...Will her reply be, "Oh yes you will."

We live for our relationships, and we live for our connection to others. Unfortunately, these attachments can become fragmented for a variety of reasons. We would all like our lives to proceed in a smooth fashion. When they don't, the first to thing to suffer is our relationships. We sometimes attempt to control others with miniature battles. It's as though if we win the argument, then somehow we've moved closer to success.

In the long run however, every time we "win" a battle, we take something away from others. The only point of winning is to gain an advantage. When we seek advantage at the expense of others' feelings, we are damaging them. In our best relationships, both parties come away stronger, more supportive, with more understanding of each other. The evidence of our culture's patterns of associations is evident in so many short-term relationships. If the goal does not have "us" as its priority, then one of us has to suffer.

By placing the emphasis on winning the interaction, we only build shields. If it's a battle we want, then the rules change because the only outcome that counts is the score, not the depth of relationship between the two parties. Ineffective relationships continually erode in terms of respect and integrity. With every interaction and every relationship, we need to examine if it's important for *me* to make gains at the expense of *us*.

If the only intention we have in a relationship is to gain power over the other person, then that relationship is surely doomed. We can't force someone into love. When we are in relationships where we are feeling like someone is trying to control us (instead of work with us), we can only grow in resentment. Most of us can relate to this because we've been in a job or a family or a situation where there was an enormous abuse of power. In all cases, the abused person (the oppressed person) can only dream of getting out.

We need to examine and think about the ways we seek advantage. We can do it overtly with harsh treatment, meanness, and instilling fear. Other times it's done with covert manipulation in the form of gossip, the defamation of another's reputation, sarcasm, and passive-aggressive manipulation.

We also need to be aware of the numerous ways where oppressive roles in families cause one person to do more work than the other. Again, the only reaction it can generate is resentment. Oppression of others occurs in a multitude of different ways and in a multitude of relationships. It is done in homes, the workplace, and in numerous daily exchanges. It is important for us to ask constantly—are my needs being met with others? Or, at the expense of others? Or, at my expense? Are other people your tools to get your job done? Or are they human beings?

We are beginning to understand this concept in educational systems, and those schools that place an emphasis on how we relate are reducing aggression and violence. We know that peer mediation and peer courts work. We know that conflict resolution and character education programs really make changes in children. The same holds true for families that use these principles. Family counseling can be useful in times of domestic war. There is more production, joy, and peace and less stress in a democracy than in a dictatorship. Most family therapists suggest that when there is a significant problem in the home, we need to have "family council." For example, if we need our two teenagers to help more with little duties, we know how well it works when we snap off a few lines like, "I'm sick and tired of living with a bunch of pigs!" There is a much greater chance for mutual understanding when the family sits down and says, "We've all become very busy, and it's unfair that any one person in this family should be another's keeper. If we all worked together..."

One-Minute Reflection: Relating

When I am in a conflict with others, what percent of the time do I spend thinking—

___How can I hit 'em back?

___How can I prove I'm right?

___What will I do to come out on top?

___What's the best method to hit 'em where it hurts?

___Am I teaching my children to hit back?

Or—

___How can I improve our relationship?

___How can we talk about our tension?

___Am I willing to swallow my pride so we can move forward?

___Are we moving toward a common goal?

___As a mature adult in this equation, am I taking responsibility for nurturing us toward this goal?

Build Healthy Dependency

As I would not be a slave, so I would not be a master. This expresses my idea of democracy.

Abraham Lincoln

Maria looked like she had just finished running a marathon. She appeared tired, beaten, and weary—the state of her relationship with her family was draining the life out of her. She described a recent episode with her son when she confronted him in regard to not doing household chores. "The instant that my thirteen-year-old said it, I realized so much of what I had done wrong. 'That's women's work!' was his reply. I had just sat my family down and told them that we would all start doing our own laundry."

She went on to describe how her fifteen-year-old son, and her ten-year-old daughter had also grown accustomed to a lifestyle. Maria also had come to realize that it was her fault, as sad as it was, but she was responsible for this lifestyle where she became the family doormat. She told me, "As a single mother, I had not realized how my sense of self-worth had become so twisted. I somehow believed that as long as I did everything for others, that we would all have mutual respect. I now realize that nothing could be further from the truth, and when my son said the 'women's work' line, it was like being conked over the head with a twenty-pound skillet. It hurt. It was also the proof of how my children had come to see me in this relationship. I began to realize the insane things I would do for my kids. I was the one to cook, clean, do the laundry, clean the yard, and virtually every other household task. Of course, my belief was that if I did everything for them—they would love me! I even remember pouring cereal and milk in a bowl for my fifteen-year-old one morning. I thought to myself—could there be a more dysfunctional relationship than this?"

Maria's situation is all too common; she created a family norm that weakened others rather than strengthen them. The other extreme is to be "Drill Sergeant Mom" where we beat fear into children as they live life here in the family barracks, but this style of living is equally ineffective.

In Maria's case, she eventually hit her wall and pulled her children into family therapy. What she found was that there would be some new stress in the house, but the old stress of disrespect would be gone. Maria described her outcome, "So here I was with three able-bodied kids who lived the life of luxury with their in-house maid. I couldn't resent it—hell, I created it. But I realized that my enabling didn't make them stronger and more respectful, it made them weaker and (as much as I hate to say it) it made them more disrespectful. I swallowed my pride and dragged my kids into family therapy. I thought that house-work was tough. Creating mutual respect is much tougher, and having my kids responsible for sharing the house duties has been *very* tough. I've had dissension, anger, and bitterness. It's an uphill battle, and it hurts because sometimes it feels like it would be easier to just go back to doing all the work. What keeps me going is remembering something that our family therapist said, 'Do you want them bitter now while you can control the variables in the house, or miserable later in life with failed relationships that will lack mutual respect?'"

In just a few weeks, Maria said that she began to separate out the "healthy emotional dependencies" from the "you're the maid" dependencies. She also said that the greatest reward was that the new phase of her family life all of a sudden had some new twists, "I nearly fell to the floor one day when my son thanked my daughter for helping him with the dishes."

When we are in painful relationships, it's common for us to dwell on what's causing the pain rather than what a healthy mu-tual dependent relationship should look like. Healthy families, workplaces, and marriages all have the same emotional dynamics. No one is abusing or taking advantage of others, and all members have healthy expressions of gratitude for one another. Many of us adults can relate to that boss who makes our life miserable, and that boss for whom we would walk over burning coals. The difference is in the sincere mutual respect. The parents who have the most difficult time are more interested in controlling every-thing in their child's life rather than collaborating *with* the child toward mutual goals. It may be the most difficult task in leadership, teaching, and parenting. It takes a strong heart, patience, time, a plan, and the ability to drop the ego.

In order to develop collaborative relationships, we need to embrace dependency as an everyday value. Over time, *dependency* is a concept that has been given a bad name. It's as though we've come to believe that leaning on others is a sign of weakness. We constantly depend on one another for material things, and we have to be okay with a healthy mutual leaning for our emotional needs as well. As far as physical needs, we trust hundreds of people to do their jobs, and the result is a comfortable lifestyle. For instance, in a hundred years it would be impossible to know everything there is to know about cars, medicine, house construction, etc. It would be nearly impossible to have many of the luxuries we enjoy without healthy mutual dependencies. The problem is that despite all of the comforts that we have, many people are still dying of loneliness because the area of mutual dependency that we disregard is that of emotional dependency. What good are all these objects that we can provide for one another when a person is considering taking a razor to her wrists? Or, when he's given up hope and holds a gun to his head, or stands on the edge of a cliff?

As we've heard plenty of times, there's no instruction book that comes with life, and all too often we have no chapter to turn to when we are despondent and alone. A newborn child is totally dependent. We are needed for everything. As we raise children, we hope incrementally and slowly to build their life-skills. In time they will learn to clean their own bathrooms, do their own laundry, make their own meals, transport themselves, wake themselves, and support themselves. In the end we hope to have a strong human being who has healthy interdependent relationships and completes tasks, and meets many other people's needs while also meeting his or her own.

We also hope that our children can be resilient, roll with the punches, and deal with the challenges that life hands them. Most importantly however, they need to develop healthy mutual respect where no one is abusing power over another and all parties are trying to build collaborative and respectful boundaries. In these relationships, each party holds the other's welfare as a top priority.

Many of our relationships involve an authoritative figure. Parents have a right to establish the house rules, but that role doesn't mean they have the right to be abusive. At the other end of the spectrum, it doesn't mean that the person who is responsible should be a door mat.

Emphasize Truthful Communication

> **That old law about an eye for an eye leaves us all blind.**
>
> **Martin Luther King**

The woman seemed to have her hands full as she pushed a stroller through the mall. The shops were crowded, and like many of us she looked like she was finishing her holiday shopping. Her daughter appeared to be about three years old and asked a question in a small mousy voice. Most of the people around her could not hear the question but it was hard not to notice the mother's response, "You just sit there and shut up!"

The three year old then answered with a reply of her own, "No! You shut up!"

The mother instantly reacted by leaning over the front of the stroller and slapping the girl's face and shouting, "Don't you talk to me that way!" She then pushed the stroller down the mall, and we could hear the echoes of a crying girl being pushed away.

It's obvious that this kind of treatment is severe, but these kinds of exchanges are so common that we've come to accept them as the norm in our culture. We've grown to accept rudeness, harshness, and abuse as everyday occurrences. Snappy retorts are the only mode of communication that many adults know. They use them *not only* with their family but also with clerks, co-workers, and loved ones—all the time wondering why their needs are not being met.

At the top of many lists of "Qualities of Healthy People," or "Self-actualized," or "Strong Relationships," we find the catch phrase "Good Communicator" that everyone thinks he or she is. In reality, it seems many adults lack this quality. It seems as though we want everyone else to be a square communicator with us, but we so often fall into the trap of not saying what we want to say.

We experience many situations where people haven't thought about whether or not their behaviors will result in a collaborative outcome, but they stay focused on the "eye for an eye" mentality. There are other forms of dishonest communication that happen around us everyday, when people are too weak to say what they want. They can't confront others, so they tear them down with gossip behind their backs. When they feel mistreated by waiting too long in line, they snap at innocent people. When they are frustrated with others not living up to their standards, they throw out sarcastic lines that have no other purpose than to "make you feel my pain."

Absolutely none of these methods of verbal exchanges has any positive effect on our relationships and our lives. We lash out in our inability to think about how to create a healthy line of communication. We take what's most important to another and try to beat him down with it. We steal another's pride, we willfully hurt others, and we cause others distress. In doing so, we create a culture of cheap shots. Sometimes the shots are so subtle that we don't even recognize how they have woven themselves into the fabric of our everyday lives.

In one of my first jobs several years ago, I worked with a supervisor who was mean-spirited, and I suppose I felt sorry for her in many ways. I was out of the office for three days on personal business, and on the day I returned, I was sitting in my office talking to another person when she stopped by and stuck her head in the doorway. "Oh, hello Steve, I didn't know you still worked here..." She smiled, turned, and walked down the hallway.

At the time, I remember experiencing a lot of stress. Not unlike many other people in these situations, I became more distressed, and couldn't immediately understand why I felt this way. My supervisor had a knack of never saying what she wanted to say. She would use sarcasm, gossip, snide remarks, and for the most part, she was curt with nearly everyone. I always wondered what kept her from saying what she wanted to say. Why couldn't she say, "I'm disappointed...Where have you been? I wish I could have had your help for the last few days...It was difficult not to have you around for a few days..." I'm sure she was inconvenienced at my absence, but I always wondered how people become such poor communicators.

For those of us who have been around people like her, common sense tells us that we shouldn't let them get to us, but it's difficult because they are hurtful. If we can get past these people and *not* join them in their tactics, we can become stronger and more insightful. I emphasize this in my violence prevention workshops. The most important question that I ask educators and parents is, "Is it any wonder why our youth become petty, sarcastic, and say rotten things to one another?" All we have to do is look to the head of a classroom or the head of a family to see some of our poorest examples. Many teachers don't realize how they are lashing out in anger when they sarcastically say things like, "Well Bobby it looks like we are well prepared today! Well Julie, we sure are working hard aren't we? Hey Ernie, it's nice to see you on time again!"

As responsible adults, we need to be the best communicators in the system. I was in a classroom once when a teacher became frustrated with a student and decided to humiliate publicly an unprepared student by asking, "Joey, what grade are you in, and what semester is this?" When the student answered "seventh grade? Second semester." The teacher became angry and said, "Don't get smart with me!"

We hear it with coaches, teachers, parents, and administrators all the time. We know the difference between joking and sarcasm. Off the cuff remarks and sarcasm are cheap shots. We need to stop and listen to the coach who is screaming at his team, "Are you trying to make my life miserable?" Or, the teacher saying "We're really paying attention today aren't we Billy?" Or, the parent remarking sarcastically, "It sure is great to have kids who do so much work!"

It's no wonder children become belligerent with such role models. I walk around the school during recess and free time, and I realize how abusive our culture can be. The trash talking and the remarks are not only inappropriate—it seems like the entire environment is raising its level of stress.

Adults need to practice saying what they want to say, rather than verbally beating the kids up. All we have to do is look at how it works on us. When my supervisor was mean to me and said, "I didn't know you still worked here..." All I could do for the next hour was think of the snide remarks that I could have said back to her, *I was just wondering the same about you... Yes, at least some of us still work around here..."* but I realized that it's too easy to meet meanness with meanness, and if we are aggressive with others, we will often get the aggression in return. Is this what we really want with our lives? Going back to the example of the three-year-old in the stroller, she learned exactly that by responding to her mother, "No, you shut up!"

Adults can consciously decide to be vulgar, rude, and angry. Children, on the other hand will only be able to act in a manner that has been modeled to them. Saying what we want to say has to become a priority, and we need to reflect on our motives. Ineffective patterns of communication have ulterior motives. After someone has been verbally abusive with us, we aren't thinking, *wow, I must have hurt him, thanks for that hurtful comment back! I'll be much better next time!* It *never* happens. Verbal abuse only incites anger in others.

None of us is born with the "ineffective communication" gene. It's a habit we learn, and if we want children and our loved ones to react differently to us, then we need to approach them differently. In learning to relate to others, we need to develop a format for dealing with our unmet needs. The first place I start with anyone (adults and children alike) is to reflect on "constructive requests." Sarcasm, drill sergeant screams, and iron dictatorships produce destructive requests.

We need to practice and reinforce appropriate communication, and much of it is simpler than we think. I do this by having people rehearse saying what they need by developing four pieces of the message. These four pieces are essential for a constructive request:

1.   **Non-blamefully, describe the unmet need or problem.**

2.   **State your congruent feeling.**

3.   **Describe the tangible effect it has on your relationship.**

4. **Tell the other person what can be gained from a mutual understanding and a collaborative change.**

For example, if I am married to a sloppy spouse, dropping sarcastic hints will only make her blood boil when I say, "It sure is hard to find a clean dish in this house, but I suppose it wouldn't be so tough if I lived with someone who could occasionally put a dish in the dishwasher!"

By using a constructive request, I could do things differently and try to build our relationship rather than destroy it when I say, "Honey I need to talk to you for a second. When I see the dishes in the sink, I feel frustrated because of all the time it takes to keep the kitchen clean, and I think we would have a lot more time for both of us and a lot less tension if we simply did the dishes every time we use them instead of letting them pile up."

Notice that in a constructive message the first part is a **non-blameful description** and *does not* include the word *you*. If I say "when *you* leave *your* socks on the floor…when *you* leave the kitchen in a mess…when *you* leave the cap off the tooth-paste…" Using the word *you* instantly puts others on the defense. It's better to leave it out, and own your observation—"When I see clothes all over the floor…"

In the second part, **your congruent feelings**, notice that it doesn't say, "It *makes* me feel…" Rather, it simply says, "I feel…" The reason for this is again, that we need to own our feelings. The dishes don't make us feel anything. We choose to feel this way about the dishes in the sink.

The third part is the **tangible effect** on me or us. Most often this is *time* or *money*. If we are the family maid, it is not only unfair, it is time consuming. If someone is destroying something with his temper, it costs us money. This is a tough part of a constructive request because if you can't find this **tangible effect** then maybe it's you who needs the change, not others. For example, I remember one morning when my children were about nine- and ten-years old and my house was like the Ringling Brothers Circus. There were kids, cats, dogs, stereos blaring, and other assorted chaotic occurrences as the whole neighborhood gaggle of kids skipped through my house. I entered the room and tried to read the paper. I felt a little fussy, so I took a deep breath and thought about how I would say something to my two boys. The first two parts of the message (nonblameful, and feelings) would be easy, "Boys, when I hear all this ruckus, I feel frustrated and stressed out and…" I couldn't come up with the tangible effect. Were they destroying the house? Did their noise cause me more work? Did life under the big top cause me to lose precious time? I realized that if I couldn't come up with the tangible effect on me, then I simply needed to leave the room, and perhaps I was just in a bad mood. They weren't doing anything wrong; as a matter of fact they were being great rambunctious kids. If I had yelled at them or lashed out at them, it would have been only an extension of my own mood and served no useful purpose. I simply took my paper and read it elsewhere.

Constructive requests have numerous benefits. They are respectful—because we don't attack. There are reflective—because we have to verbalize our feelings. And, they are moving us toward how our relationship can be more productive and mutually considerate. As we exercise constructive requests, we will also experience less resentment. If we say what we want to say (even if it doesn't always create a civil response), at least we won't have to obsess over *what could have been done.* Resentment is a form of self-torture. Grudges have a tendency to hurt ourselves more than our targets. As William Walton once said, "To carry a grudge is like being stung to death by one bee." It's pretty obvious that miserable people spend their lives being stung to death repeatedly.

Most of all, however, constructive requests teach us that a civil approach is the most constructive approach. It's teaching a child how to respond to others in a civilized society. If the child learns that she will be smacked across the cheek when she says something that upsets others, then she will grow up with an "old west" mentality—if someone upsets me, pull out my six-shooter and gun him down. These are kids who are aggressive in school, and who usually eventually batter their own spouses and children.

One-Minute Reflection: Truthful Communication

Life is often in disarray—a long line, dishes piled high in the sink, people not pitching in to help, a rude co-worker, an angry relative, how do you typically respond? Take a moment and think about an interaction with someone else in the past week that brought you stress. Of course not all situations are the same, an angry child may be dealt with differently from an angry CEO, but the emotional patterns are the same.

Do any of the following sound familiar?

__I'm better off letting things slide.

__I just need to do it myself; if you want a job done right, do it yourself.

__Keep it to yourself.

__I've been known to drop a few sarcastic hints once in a while, just to get their attention.

__They're going to get my worst side, but, hey, everyone has a bad hair day; others need to learn to live with it.

__Occasionally, it works best to let it out, get in someone's face, and let 'em have it.

For any of the above, the pattern is the same: are you typically angry? passive? aggressive? Do you respond in a way that brings personal distress? In other words, does the situation tend to eat away at you for a lengthy period of time? We are all confronted with situations where we wish we could have been more effective in communicating our needs, and we need to ask ourselves: what keeps me from making a constructive request? pride? ego? hate to lose? hate injustice? people need to get a dose of their own medicine? fear? In order to reduce our stress, we have to decide consciously if there is a way for us to create a constructive request.

You were asked to think about a stressful situation above. Sit down and write out a constructive response using all four parts listed in the previous section (see page 152–3). Then decide if you are in a position to use them. If you are not, then are you willing to let it go? What's keeping you from moving on?

> **If things are not working, ask yourself, "In what way am I creating this? In what way can I change this? What is the lesson?"**
>
> **Wayne Dyer**

There are seven words that I hear at every violence prevention or parenting workshop. "How can I get my kids to...?" A frustrated teacher or parent has a situation where nothing has worked. What follows the seven words are a variety of needs, but each one has the same preface, "How can I get my kids to—clean their room...not sass me...get their homework done...not pick on their brother...stop hitting other kids...etc. etc."

These are all situations where an adult wants to create a positive change in a child but hasn't found a method or a technique that works. In nearly all of these cases, I can guarantee you that the adult is doing at least one of three things that *don't* work. It's important to examine what's not working as well as what works. There are three major mistakes that we make in parenting and teaching that never result in positive changes;

1. Staying focused on what we don't want.

2. Rewarding incompetence.

3. Mixing punishment with rewards.

When something is not working, we need to look at all of the variables that allow the behavior to occur. First, we need to stop obsessing on what *we don't want*. Many teachers and parents often say, "I feel like I spend my whole life telling my kids to stop what they are doing." The key to changes in anyone is to **focus on what you want him to do—not on what you don't want him to do!** If we watch masterful teachers and parents, we will notice that they *don't* spend their days screaming at kids, and always telling them *don't* or *stop!* We will notice that when an inappropriate behavior occurs, they focus on what they want done. Instead of saying, "Stop pushing him!" They say, "When we are in line, we keep our hands to ourselves."

By continually dishing out the "Thou shalt nots," the best we can hope for is to stop certain behaviors, but we can't move anyone toward the appropriate behavior.

When my son was five years old, I remember when I said to him, "I don't want you to climb up on that counter and get into those cookies! We're going to have dinner soon." My son nodded and indicated that he understood. A little while later, I returned to find cookies missing, and evidence of the crumbs on the counter. When I confronted him with "Did you climb up there and get those cookies?" He continually responded with "No..." I finally asked, "You're telling me you didn't eat the cookies?" He nodded then indicated "yes." Now I was really frustrated because I felt like I had been lied to. My son said, "I didn't climb up there, I hopped up there!"

A "thou shalt not" is often useless, because we are looking for angles to get our needs met. Even adults do it, "Thou shalt not steal." *Well, it depends on what you mean by steal...this was just a little pilfering...they are only pencils from the office...* Even the Good Lord might have been more successful by issuing a commandment, "Thou shalt respect the property of others..."

"Thou shalt nots" are always arguable. How many times have we told children, "I thought I told you not to hit him!" And, their reply is, "I didn't, I tapped him...I bumped him..." We would be better off from the beginning to think of what we want, "we need to keep our hands to ourselves."

With children, we need always to focus on what we want them to do. Inadequate teachers will stand by the door screaming and flashing the light switch saying, "We have to stop making noise now!" Ineffective parents will beat their children and ground them every time they are fighting with each other.

Masterful teachers establish the norms early for their classrooms by describing what a "listening and learning" position looks like, instead of complaining about the fidgeting child. Effective parents do more than give extra punishment every time a sibling beats up another sibling; they try to support empathic feelings for one another. Most of us remember the times in our own youth when we were given extra work or a spanking when we were mean to our siblings. So, mom grounds us for smacking little brother and what did we learn? We certainly didn't learn to be emotionally responsible for our siblings. We only learned to smack little brother when mom is not around.

The most useful aspect of learning to *focus on what we want* is that we stop complaining. If all we can do is scream about what we don't want, we adopt a pattern of seeing the world for its problems, not its solutions. A focus on solutions makes us develop plans. It also empowers us to make changes in life. Change is a lot more fun than self-persecution.

The second major mistake we make when trying to build strong collaborations is **rewarding incompetence**. All of us are capable of doing this either knowingly or unknowingly. We often do this in our families and in our jobs and each time we do, we are being personally irresponsible. Every time we support another's irresponsible behavior, we are in fact irresponsible ourselves.

Rewarding incompetence is a perfect scenario for a martyr, or the perpetually angry person, and in some cases she would prefer to revel in her own self-induced misery than to correct the problem. Rather than collaborating on a plan, and holding children responsible for "not leaving dishes, cups, and coats strewn around the house," she prefers to do the work, then moan about it.

We are also capable of doing this as adults. In one of my courses we were discussing "roles" in our families, and a woman in her mid-forties described how she had to leave a dozen notes for her husband every night that she came to class, "Turn the oven to 450...the salad is in the blue dish...Joey needs a bath... help Sarah with her history paper...put the laundry in the dryer—but don't start another load—I haven't separated the darks and whites yet..."

Another student in my class told her, "You only need one note, 'Tonight you're on your own, good luck! All my love!'"

She then indicated, "Oh no, I couldn't do that. He would just screw up the dinner; he's done laundry before—and totally messed it up. I can't trust him to do anything if I don't tell him."

The woman didn't realize that she was responsible for putting the "dys" in a dysfunctional family. How many intense years of training does it take to learn to do a load of laundry? How many literature classes do you need to prepare you to read and comprehend the back of a macaroni and cheese box? By spoon-feeding others the things they should be doing for themselves, we are as irresponsible as they are. It's one thing to have a collaborative agreement, "You start cooking lunch, and I'll shovel the walks," and it's another to say, "I'll be your lifelong house-keeper."

Sometimes the mentor in the relationship has simply lost patience. If you are teaching a child to wipe off the table properly, demonstrate it, then sit on your hands. All too often we are compelled to say "Here, just give me the rag and I'll do it!" The result is a child who learns that *I don't have to learn it...I don't have to pick up after myself...I don't have to remember my homework or to brush my teeth...Mom will remember it for me!* The child may also learn that no matter what he or she does—it is wrong or never good enough. As a result the child never develops confidence and competence in the presence of the adult. He is the kid who continually looks into the stands during soccer games and debate competitions. He is self-conscious and has a predisposition to self-doubt. He goes through life with a myriad of twisted self-messages about his personal sense of self-worth.

Every time we reward incompetence, we also weaken the system. When was the last time we saw an incompetent co-worker get shuffled off to another task and not be held accountable? The result was a weaker system. Our relationships and families work the same way.

The third major mistake we make that keeps us from collaboration is **mixing punishments with rewards**. Whenever we mix them together, we are controlling the variables of an environment in an irresponsible manner

Punishment is different from consequences. To experience *consequences* for my behavior means I have to work on getting it right, fixing it. A seat in the corner, or a beating—for the lack of blind obedience has little to do with fixing a problem or generating solutions. In most cases, it's more about the person in the position of authority appeasing his or her anger needs.

Imagine what it would be like if you had a bad day on your job and you went out to the parking lot and couldn't find your company car. Soon your boss appears and puts her arm around your shoulder and says, "Oh I'm sorry, I forgot to tell you, since you had such a bad day, we took away your car."

Imagine if you had a week where a few things didn't go right on the job and when you came home you found out that half of your bank account was gone. When you asked, the bank manager said, "Oh I'm sorry, since you didn't have such a great week, we took your money away."

If these things happened to us, we would lose all our motivation to work hard on the job. We would initially be excited to earn our money, but later we would not trust the system of payment because it would unpredictably take away our rewards at different times.

We would despise a world where all of our rewards also became our punishments, so why do we so often create this kind of world for our children? Certainly, consequences may be necessary when we are accountable for our actions, such as breaking the law or a serious violation of others, but not when we make mistakes in our everyday lives; we enjoy having a nurturing guide to help us work on getting it right. Think about those times when you learned something on a job. What motivated you? Someone who punished you every step of the way? Someone who made us deathly afraid to make mistakes in front of? Or, someone who was patient and worked in successive steps to lead us to competency?

If you constantly lived under a fear of punishment for every behavior you were involved in, you would begin to think—*why try at all? Why should I invest myself in something that I know will be a trip of misery? Why should I go after something that I believe has a greater chance of robbing me of my dignity than nourishing it?* In the long run, when we are constantly in fear of what we may lose in a situation, instead of focusing on what we may gain, we grow resentful. If we lived with these constant threats to our harmony, it would drive us crazy! It only makes sense that our children will react the way we do—if they are afraid of making mistakes in our presence, they will avoid us like the plague.

Think about how often we smother children's motivation by allowing them to earn a reward, and then hold the reward hostage. For example if we said, "If you have a good week, you get to go to the zoo!" Then after a good week we say, "You've had a good week, good job! Now we are going to the zoo!" Then when Friday comes we say, "No! You had a bad morning so we are staying home, but you can try next week to work toward another trip, this time we may go to the amusement park!"

If any person (child or adult) cannot trust a system of reinforcement, it will not serve as a motivation A golden rule for keeping a child's sanity—keep the rewards and punishments separate. Mixing them will only serve to make the child distrustful, complacent, very angry, and soon see the world as a place of false promises.

I once knew a family that consistently (but unknowingly) made their children crazy with the mixing of punishment with rewards. On one occasion their two elementary school-age children were doing well in school and the parents sat them down and told them, "As your reward for your good grades, we are going to Disney over our spring break this year!" This is a dream come true for two children in their elementary school years, but what they didn't expect was the torture that would ensue over the next three months. Every time their father was mad at them, he would hold the vacation over their heads, "If you don't get that room cleaned...if you don't get that homework done...then we are not going to Disney!" Soon, Mom joined in as well, "if you don't get those dishes done...then we are not going to Disney!"

I don't think that the parents realized how abusive they had become toward their children. After about a month of this insanity the young boy started screaming, "I don't even want to go on the stupid vacation!" By the time they were ready to leave, the young girl repeatedly said, "I'm sick of hearing about this stupid vacation, I hope we never have another one." From the look in her eye, I could tell that she would probably be happier if she could slap Snow White silly.

These attempts at discipline are quite common. The one in control of the variables is doing nothing more than torturing others and playing the martyr game—"Here I am saving for this great vacation for you—and this is the thanks I get!" *I am so damn wonderful and everyone else is mean, thoughtless, and incompetent.*

Each time we abuse this disciplinary power, we sever one more connection between ourselves and the person we are working with—and it's all driven from insecurity. We have to separate out consequences from punishment. If a child knows that he can't play until he gets the room cleaned, it's the same as an adult knowing that he can't get paid unless he goes to work, and he can't retain his driver's license unless he abides by the rules of the road. In all cases we knew the consequences because we know the rules. If you are pulled over for a traffic violation—you know the consequences ahead of time. You are sure what will happen if you are pulled over for speeding, it isn't arbitrary—the cop doesn't pull you over and say, "Guess what pal, you were clocked doing 70 miles per hour—you don't get to go out with your wife to dinner tomorrow—and I want you at my house in the morning to clean my toilet."

When we do these things to children, the best we can hope for is a child who begins to hate his home and the person in charge of it. If you needed something from an adult, is this the way you would treat him? "Grandma, if you don't stop fidgeting in line, then we're not going to the Barry Manilow concert tonight!"

We need to rethink these useless threats, especially if we want to preserve our relationships. The other problem with these arbitrary punishments is that others will begin to see us as deceitful (full of empty promises). Children need to trust their environment and know that their efforts are respected and that they are not held hostage.

Just like children's mistakes, most of our mistakes are not done with malice; we are simply trying to survive. If a child acts out, misbehaves, or makes a mistake, most of the time it is simply an extension of his survival techniques! She is *not* doing this because she *wants to push your buttons, agitate you, or upset you* personally. Personalizing it only makes you a self-persecutor. Kids are simply trying to get their needs met, and they need our love, care, and compassion to nurture them into behaving in better ways to get their needs met.

Making Collaboration Part of Our Everyday Lives
Giving Others What They Deserve

> **All relationships have disagreements, but not all relationships have battles. Therein lies the difference in respect, nurturing, and collaboration. With every disagreement, we either gain more mutual respect or lose it.**

Weak egos are consumed with defending their inappropriate behavior. We say to ourselves, "That co-worker of mine *deserved* my wrath...that person on the highway *deserved* my middle finger...my kids *had that beating coming to them*...I showed that store clerk a thing or two—she *had it coming*!" In each of these cases we are defending our egos, by saying, "I'm still a good person…it's just that these people need to be taught a lesson." At these times we have to realize that we are doing nothing to create a collaborative world.

We buy into a philosophy that says, "I will give a person only what he deserves." For all of those times that we are inconvenienced, treated rudely, or treated harshly, can we respond in a manner that reflects what we preach? I've seen teachers with classrooms loaded with abusive, attention deficit, emotionally disturbed children who are constantly on a mission to act out. So what do the children deserve? If we are waiting for children to act in a manner that pleases us so that they can get what we believe they *deserve,* we're going to be waiting until the moon turns blue. It's clear that the teachers and parents who have the greatest progress with these children are the ones who are giving them *more* love than most people believe they "deserve." They are handing out *more* patience than they "deserve," and *more* understanding than they "deserve." The same holds true for our everyday interactions with adults. When we are confronted with a rude person, we get greater results when we treat him with *more* kindness he deserves. This is what separates the person who talks about character and the person who lives it.

The miracle is in how quickly one person can make a difference. Have you ever noticed when you are dealing with someone who's had a very frustrating day and you approach her with kindness and respect, how a change comes over her? When we kindly ask for help, or are nice to her, it changes the way she treats us. Not all people respond immediately to kindness because there are those who revel in their misery, but if given an opportunity to make a difference, doesn't it make sense that we should take the chance? Especially if we see ourselves as caring people! The worst thing we can do in any relationship is to see the personal victory as more important than the team victory. With every disagreement, we either gain more mutual respect or lose it.

Hope is one of the most beautiful things to live for. It only comes when we share power with others, not hold it over them.

One-Minute Reflection: Collaboration

When collaboration becomes central to one's philosophy of life, we remove stress, become more productive and valuable to others. Most importantly, we bring greater meaning to our lives. The following are questions we need to ask ourselves each day of our lives. At the end of a typical day this week, reflect on the following questions. "Am I satisfied with the collaboration in my relationships?"

1. Will my family, personal relationships, and working relationships all be stronger at the end of the day? Or weaker?

2. What presence do I bring to my day? How do people react when I enter a room? Do they tighten up? Quiet down? Look for corners?

3. What purpose do I bring to my day? Is it to make our lives better? or just my life better?

4. Do I try to motivate by giving? or only by taking?

5. Do I really have an "open door?" How approachable am I? Do I truly enjoy building trust?

6. Do I sometimes relish that role of having power over others? "I showed them... I got the best of that one... I won that argument... I got the last word in on that one..."

7. If I mistreat others, did I try to rationalize my way out of it? Defend myself? "Anyway I treated all the important people well..." Is there any thing that is keeping me from seeing all others as important?

The Journey To True Wisdom Can only be Traveled with a Heart that Embraces Human Differences

I adjusted my overhead projector and placed the last slide in my notebook. The principal then asked the crowd if they had any questions for me. For the past hour I had gone over several strategies for staying connected to our children. The participants were a group of parents who had children in junior high school. A foot of snow had fallen that day, and there were only about twenty-five parents. They braved the cold winter night to venture to the school to get some ideas for working with their children.

In the front row sat a mother who looked to be about thirty-five years old. Throughout the evening she sat attentively, and every time I looked at her she seemed to be fixed on every word I said. She slowly raised her hand to about shoulder height. I pointed to her and asked, "Yes, you have a question?"

Her head dipped momentarily then she looked up. She paused and tried to speak but the words weren't coming. Her head went down again then she looked up at me again. She brought her hands to her face to wipe the tears from her cheeks. Her lower lip quivered as she summoned the courage to speak in front of other parents. "My daughter…" She gulped and started again. "My daughter…is one of the most beautiful people I've ever known. She grew up with this bubbly personality and this smile that could knock you off your feet…" The woman stopped and wiped more tears away then spoke again. "In the past year her life has slowly gone down hill, and I don't know what to do.

She doesn't want to go to school, she is depressed, and it seems she has no friends."

In the next few minutes she described how her daughter was popular in elementary school but how vicious her junior high school experience had become. Some of the girls in the school had created cliques. It seemed like these cliques summoned every malicious and nasty quality that a teenage girl could possess. Computer instant messenger rumors were started about her daughter providing sex for boys, and it snowballed into meanness and the destruction of her reputation as well as her esteem. Her daughter now sat at home and cried, wrote suicide notes, and sunk into crying spells. "How does all this happen to a sweet girl in such a short period of time? What can I do for her Dr. Birchak?"

With only five minutes left in the evening session I had about a hundred things I would have liked to have said, but like the girl's mother, in so many ways I felt helpless. Words were not enough. A couple pieces of advice in five minutes would not change her situation.

The case was a mirror image from one week earlier. Two parents had shared with me that they had a son in the seventh grade. He was blessed with flaming red hair. Because of that hair he was tortured emotionally day after day. The most popular kid in the school (big, good looking, strong, loud, and insecure) would knock his lunch tray out of his hands and call him "carrot head boy." He sat at home and cried as his mother asked the same question, "What can I do for him Dr. Birchak?"

I remember my own childhood with the messages of, "Learn to toughen up...it won't last forever...the boys are just being boys...girls will be girls...some kids just bring it on themselves..." And of course we know who is saying all of these things. They are coming from the parents who are happy that

169

it's not their children in that situation. They silently turn their heads, thankful it's *not my kid.*

What these parents don't understand is that *it is your kid.* By neglecting to help the mean kids, we are doing them a tremendous disservice. They are the ones who will grow up without a conscience, unable to develop fruitful relationships, and unable to gain wisdom because they believe they "hold all the cards" in regard to the purpose of life. They separate themselves from others, look down on the less fortunate, and do everything in their power to maintain their position of privilege. In many ways, it's like a curse, and a meaningful life becomes elusive.

There are two issues at stake here. First, what is a civilized society doing to protect its children? And second, what should *all* children learn to help create a more compassionate world?

All members of any civilized society have the right to ask for protection from abuse (children and adults alike). When we have a disagreement in public we can't settle, we should have a means for arbitration. Parents and children have the right to ask—does our school have peer mediation? Peer court? Conflict resolution? Accountability for one's actions? Schools need to be a microcosm of a healthy society, not a microcosm of a lawless one. It is every person's right to pressure the system to protect its citizens, whether in a community or a school.

Both of the above cases had parents who wanted to do something. Should we call the principal? The other child's parents? How can we help? Their presence at the meeting was evidence of their investment, but they felt as if their hands were tied.

One thing is certain—we must teach our children how to defend themselves—not physically, but legally. Much of that can be developed with resilience skills, but children also need to be reassured that they live in a system where they don't have to take the law into their own hands. They need to know that they are protected by that system—an educational process that promotes peaceful relationships.

When an insane and delusional person decides to terrorize and harm others, it's clear that wiping him off the face of the earth does nothing to teach others of the virtues of promoting peace. What is needed is *not* the elimination of one who is cruel, but the education of those who are naïve. It's true that we may need force to stop that insane person in times of crisis, but that force has never been effective as a teaching tool.

We are interdependent, not independent creatures, and our source of wisdom resides in the understanding of others and not in the building of walls. All children need to learn the value of human kinship. **Kinship** is the fifth lesson in our quest for character, cooperation, and understanding. It's the lesson that looks deeply at the larger picture of peaceful relationships among human beings. It has components of many of the other lessons such as civility, the development of a social conscience, and collaborative skills. What sets it apart is this fundamental value—it's our differences that give us our greatest source of wisdom. Learning stops when we cannot accept our differences. Compassion is stifled when we become intolerant. Each time we look at our human differences and seek to place ourselves in a position of privilege, we are closing the door to another's insights, hopes, and visions. This is not to say that we should not seek to improve our lives by reaching for all that the world has to offer, but if comfort or position comes at another's expense, we are supporting oppression.

Kinship is the ability to embrace human differences and to accept those differences and seek wisdom through their understanding. It includes all of those human differences that we so readily notice such as color and gender but also goes further by understanding how so many everyday practices may hurt others—just like the girl who was separated from her peers, and the red-headed boy who was hurt day after day. For these children, it sets the wheels in motion to look for any and all differences and later to view them as threats. Soon it will include color, religion, gender, nationality, and affiliation.

If we accept these as normative behaviors, then we are supporting aggression, and we are teaching hostility as an appropriate problem-solving mechanism. The children who practice these behaviors are learning that separation, hatred, and oppression are not only appropriate but also *essential* for their well-being.

Kinship is the ability to see the larger picture of social justice. This not only provides collective security but is also the foundation for all objectively valid human values. Children who learn intolerance, bullying, prejudice, and bigotry are on their way to becoming tomorrow's tools for unrest. When children are very young, they have no prejudices. It's through ego development, habit, and education that they learn to be intolerant of others. It's these roadblocks that keep them from becoming fully functioning adults. One of our most difficult tasks is to teach kinship to those who wield influence over others. How do you teach a person to care, especially if that person doesn't believe that it is necessary and sees no inherent value in helping others. How can we work with the bully on the playground to use his influence for something greater than mere popularity? How can we teach the bigot or the sexist not to oppress others, and that there are greater rewards from cooperation than from dominance? How can we teach cooperation, if kids believe that they have more to lose in life than gain—should they begin to see others as equals?

This chapter will look at how we can develop kinship in those who are victimizing others as well as those who are victimized. First, we need to **Free Children of their Obstacles.** We learn, as we grow, to feel threatened by differences, and we need to teach children how to create an open door to seeing and analyzing those differences for what they are. In doing so, it is important to **Teach Children Differences—The Helpful Ones as Well as the Hurtful.** It isn't necessary to be accepting of every human behavior. In fact, we need to teach children how to be good problem solvers. They need to learn how to see those differences that supply us with wisdom, and to discern them from the differences that teach hatred and oppression.

Children also need to **Learn True Freedom**. Learning that we have the freedom to express ourselves doesn't mean that we are free of responsibility. We are free to choose to rise above the insanity rather than join it. We are free to choose how we can join others together. A common practice that goes against that freedom is the **Distorted Practice of Isolation.** By isolating others or isolating ourselves from others, we keep ourselves from openness, and knowledge.

We need also to realize that it is futile to overlook certain behaviors and hope children will outgrow them. We must realize that **Bully Kids become Bully Adults.** This chapter will look at the patterns of maintaining power over others, and how these separations have a tendency to continue into adulthood.

Lastly, the chapter will address our **Invitations for Camaraderie.** If we want to keep an open door for others, we need to realize that there are opportunities for kinship around every corner.

Free Children of Their Obstacles

Fear less, hope more;
Whine less, breathe more;
Talk less, say more;
Hate less, love more;
And all good things are yours.

Swedish Proverb

The biggest obstacles that adults face in their personal happiness are their decisions about how they will view life. Adults have made up their minds about what they want to fear, complain about, become selfish about, or hate. Children have not made up their minds, and it adults who stand at their crossroads guiding them in one direction or another.

It doesn't take much to influence a child in one direction or the other. Hope can be stifled by a few rogue hostile people, as is evident by acts of aggression in our world. Laziness and self-persecution come about by watching a subculture of complainers, trash-talkers, and self-centered "heroes" in our society. Our emphasis on praising the boisterous results in less time devoted to *listening* to the wealth of wisdom that our world has to offer. And above all, our focus on *me* has resulted in the decline of small acts of kindness that contribute to our day-to-day happiness in our relationships.

In the battle against intolerance, we are seduced by a new definition of wealth. Our job is to nurture a transition away from materialistic wealth and back to an appreciation of relational wealth. Without this human value of relational wealth, our children (and adults) are unskilled in the art of love, caring, and the acceptance of others. Some may have great potential for intelligence, others may have financial success, and others may even have popularity brought on by a charismatic quality. Their ignorance however, will grow into a miserable relationship with life if it does not include an ability to accept differences between themselves and others. Their true lack of education is in the area of human compassion.

Helen Keller once said, "The highest result of education is tolerance." Tolerance allows us to seek wisdom. Wise people are constantly seeking something outside themselves, a new angle to see things, a different way to perceive things—all for the purpose of answering the questions of—*How can I bring greater relief to a world that suffers so much? How can I bring greater joy to a world that hurts others so much? How can I bring greater love to a world that often turns to apathy?*

Tolerance of differences results in the realization that each life is capable of something greater than itself. By freeing children of the shackles of hostility that emerge from racism, sexism, oppression, and prejudice, we remove their most burdensome obstacles to happiness. The greatest threat to humanity is not some new weapon; it is that weapon in the hands of an intolerant person.

To become a strong adult, a child must see adults modeling an acceptance of differences. A child must develop an understanding of what irritates us into these destructive patterns. Carl Jung once said, "Everything that irritates us about others can lead us to an understanding of ourselves." We tend to gravitate toward intolerance if we see human differences as threats. The greatest thing we can ever do with our differences is not to pound the other into agreement, but offer a place to discuss them. For all of the grief that a country like the United States suffers in terms of its perceptions in this world, one of its greatest qualities is that it offers a forum for the discussion of these differences.

A rabbi, a priest, a minister, a moslem, and an atheist can all sit at the same table and discuss these very issues without fear of retribution.

We need to help our children to avoid the glorification of "might is right." We should never fight to even a score, or fight simply to flex our muscles. We should always be ready to be passionate and battle for principles, but we should always avoid battles that are fought just for the sake of winning.

One-Minute Reflection: Obstacles

When I was growing up, I remember the day that Martin Luther King was assassinated. A boy in our neighborhood ran outside to tell us the news, "Martin Luther King was killed!" The boy then grinned and said, "My father said he had it coming and that those Negroes should take their marches elsewhere!"

As I reflect on that day, I remember that my own parents didn't share that view, but I didn't debate with this boy. I would love to tell you that I took the high road, but I didn't. I was passive. This boy was very popular and wielded a lot of power in our neighborhood. It seemed that it was more advantageous to be on his side. Obviously, if I could go back, I would do things differently. At the time, fitting in seemed to be more important. As you look back on your life, ask yourself these questions:

1.   Was I raised with obstacles that kept me from being tolerant of differences?
2.   Have I overcome those obstacles? Or do I still have an image of some human difference and see another person as less of a human being than I?
3.   We can't change history, but we can keep ourselves from repeating it. How many opportunities have you taken in the last month to talk to your children about their cliques, their groups, the biases that occur in their everyday lives?
4.   Am I passing on obstacles or eliminating them? Can I teach some personal strengths that I never had as a child?

Teach Others of Differences—
The Helpful Ones as Well as the Hurtful

> **Commandment number one of any truly civilized society is this: Let people be different.**
>
> **David Grayson**

As we teach our children to accept others, it's also important to teach them to discern between behaviors that promote the welfare of our civilization and those that harm it. We need to evolve and rise above abusive behaviors regardless of history, culture, religion, or beliefs. It doesn't matter if you are Christian, Moslem, Jewish, or Buddhist, if you are a racist you are illogical, if you are oppressive you are abusive, if you are sexist you are denying others their rights as human beings. While each of us has the right to voice our opinions, none of us has the right to deny others any of their rights to live and be free.

> **People take different roads seeking fulfillment and happiness. Just because they're not on your road, it doesn't mean they've gotten lost.**
>
> **H. Jackson Brown**

The key is not whether we accept a god, or a belief, or a religion. Rather, it is to understand that there are many paths in life. Some lead to fulfillment and others lead to human destruction. We do not have to support, condone, or accept the latter. We do however, have the duty to be open to the numerous philosophies that promote the goodness of humankind. We *do* have the right to teach children that they need to accept others, and they need to develop the skill to discern where the lines of hatred, aggression, domination, and oppression begin.

A major mistake we make is our effort to convince children that they need to act as though there are no differences between us. There are a lot of differences between us, but that doesn't mean that those differences will dictate our value as human beings. Some of our differences in beliefs may be more effective for human survival than others, and what we need to teach children is how to problem solve and use new information to make humanity stronger.

I am different from the average adult because of my physically short stature. I accept that, and I also get a kick out of being different. It has many more advantages than disadvantages. When young children are turning their heads to look at someone who is different, it is because they are interested, not because they are racist, biased, or prejudiced.

I am a grown man and I stand 4'9" tall. I find it amusing to see children who are in their shopping carts at the store and hear them exclaim, "Mommy look at the little man!" Soon they find themselves quickly whisked away by an embarrassed mom. My favorite response from children usually happens if I am sporting a beard around Christmas time. I've had several youngsters run over to me and ask, "Are you an elf?" To tell you the truth, I feel honored. I probably get the parents in trouble by promising the kids that they will get what they are asking for Christmas. "Stop lying to me! There was no elf in the cereal aisle! And he did not promise you that you will get that Malibu Barbie for Christmas!" I once heard.

If a child's head is turned by a human difference, the worst thing we can do is to pretend it doesn't exist. Heck, as adults we do the same thing. When that 7' tall man walks in the store we are staring too! (and quickly turning our heads to act like we weren't looking). It's important to recognize and celebrate our differences—not act as if they don't exist.

We are not all one size, one religion, one color, and one gender. The beauty is that we are different, and none of those differences can keep us from loving each other, caring for each other, and helping each other.

**True Freedom
is not the freedom to do as one pleases,
it is the freedom to rise above the
insanity in the world and to do what is in
the best interest of humankind.**

Teach Others True Freedom

As we drive to our jobs today we have the option to cut off *that* driver and run him off the road. Why? Because, of course *he cut me off!* We also have the option to punch our bosses, tell them where to stick it, just because—it makes us feel better. We can scream at a waitress, give the finger to a slow driver, cuss at the telemarketer, or grab a shovel and throw that pile of dog doo-doo back on my neighbor's lawn! Then we can sit back and reflect on what a fulfilling day it's been!

And why would we do these wonderful things? Because it's a free country isn't it? In fact, if we did these things, we wouldn't be free at all. We would be captive by psychopathology that goes against the very nature of humanity. To embrace truly the nature of freedom, we have to realize that free thinking, critical analysis, and strong human principles are only possible by rising above the rubble of distorted hostility and hate that we so often see.

Freedom is a wonderful thing to behold. The only positive aspect of claiming we have *no* freedom is that we don't have to be responsible for anything. We don't have to be accountable, we don't have to make choices, and we always have someone to blame. When we are behaving in narrow ways that promote violating others, we are abusing the privilege of making choices. What many hostile people fail to realize is the enormous responsibility that comes with choices. When we choose to treat others kindly *or* unkindly, there will be consequences. The question is: are we willing to be held accountable for those consequences?

All of us desire a world of bliss, peace, and love, yet we don't as often assume responsibility for our corner of it. Carl Jung once asked, "Is your thought your own, for which you are personally responsible? Or, are you a megaphone for collective opinion?" Very often, the greatest changes in human history are made not by those who conveniently follow crowds, but those who are bold enough to say, *could this crowd be wrong?*

Could part of the crowd twist a religion in order to say, "here is my license to hate others?"

Could part of the crowd lash out at someone who is different and give itself a license to hurt others? *Because, the way I read it—I can kill you and I shall be rewarded for that, according to my god, culture, country, or belief.*

Could part of the crowd mistreat others in the name of a self-serving delusion? Could these delusions result in harmful treatment of others who are doing no harm? Could the delusion result in seeing another human as less than I am? or no other reason than gender? lifestyle? religion? color? ethnicity? or background?

A great challenge lies before us. As responsible, concerned, and active adults, we need to help a generation of children to make smart choices in the face of hate sites on the internet, incivilities on the television, and the glorification of selfishness in our societal heroes. We need to analyze the moral relativism (in a legal system that's gone awry), and the delusions of hate that are supported in the name of gods.

Seeing the insanity and embracing the decision to rise above it are our humanistic ethical duties. It requires courage to make logical, common sense decisions that do not always follow the crowd. Any human being who follows a doctrine of hate is weaker than the follower on the playground who watches another child bully a weaker child. The bully is much like a terrorist. He terrorizes a small group of children, then when confronted, he claims that the larger system "is the real bully" and the system is out to make life miserable for the poor persecuted "righteous" bully. The bullying takes place for no other reason than a weak sense of self-worth. The disturbed playground bully is content to make up his own rules in order dominate his corner of the playground. The question before us is—how did this bully arrive at this mind set?

In most cases the child has learned to manipulate, bully, blame, and pitch fits because he or she has been spoon-fed a diet of anger; either it has been modeled to him or he has learned it through trial and error.

The world continues to grow smaller, and within it are numerous distractions and tests for us. With televisions and computer screens filled with information, our new task is to embrace the messages that are motivated by valid humanistic principles and to reject those which are fueled by hatred and psychopathology (even though many of these are cleverly disguised). Our true freedom must include openness to human differences, but must also allow for the rejection of dogmatic principles that serve only to injure humanity.

One-Minute Reflection: Freedom

In your lifetime, have you truly embraced your ability to be free, to rise above the insanity in the world?

___Reflect for a moment on your life and how often you've heard a sexist remark, a racist stereotype, or a religious slur.

___Have you ever heard doctrines of hostility but failed to respond to them.

___Each time this occurred what was being said between the lines? In other words, these statements often say more about the person saying them than about their intended target.

___Each time this occurred and you were passive, what was your statement of silence saying between the lines? insecurity? uncertainty? a need to fit in? fear?

Have you ever judged another lifestyle and slandered it, even though that lifestyle wasn't causing anyone any harm?

___Reflect for a minute on others' paths to fulfillment.

___Just because others don't follow your path, have you deemed theirs wrong and "this is not right for anyone?" or just "not for me."

The Distorted Practice of Isolation

> **Injustice anywhere is a threat to justice everywhere.**
>
> **Martin Luther King**

On the other side of the feeling of being connected, we should never forget the times when people purposely isolated themselves or others. In group counseling theory, the term is "subgrouping." It occurs when one member of the group feels the need to get other members of the group on his or her side. Usually this happens when a person is either challenged by the authority in the group, or is feeling the need to wrestle for the control of the group. Instead of speaking to the entire group, the subgrouper (because of insecurities) wants to turn to self-persecution to justify a need to be devious. In life there are small groups of people who may make up a minority, and they band together for a cause, but in the case of subgrouping, it's one person who creates a mini-crusade that has evolved from his insecurity.

When subgrouping occurs, those needing to move others to align may do a lot of underhanded things. Actions could be compared to the gossipy office worker. The first to gossip is generally the most insecure, needing others to take care of his or her revenge.

One of the most destructive things we can do to others is to try to get everyone else to settle our battles for us. This injustice can destroy a person's life. A false accusation, a lie spread through gossip, or a strategically devised defamation of one's character are all examples of extremely disturbed and devious people. On a larger scale, some people may create fraternities of hate against a particular group of people, then lash together subjective observations to support their conclusions. Their only goal is to foster hate. An example of this is the hundreds of hate websites that have sprung up on the internet. For those who are vulnerable (because they feel that life is treating them cruelly) these sites are fulfilling and prophetic. They create "tiers of human worth" that enable the individual to find a scale to place himself or herself all for the purposes of blame and hate.

On a smaller field, there are numerous examples of separating others from humankind when adults use "tiers of worth." Some people are just plain mean, and the saddest situations are those when an adult uses these tactics to punish a child. One common practice is to convince ourselves that the children we are working with are somehow so unique that they won't respond to the world as other humans do. For instance, you will hear adults justifying their abuse of a child by, "I know that most people don't believe in spanking, but it's the only language that *these* kids under-stand...I know that some people would say you shouldn't scream or punish these children, but it's the only thing *they understand.*

If there were any truth to the belief, it would justify the crea-tion of a screening process for people early in their lives so that we could separate them into *beatable* or *non-beatable* humans. That way we could take the guesswork out of how we need to treat others, then we could be within our rights to boast, "I only hire beatable office workers; it makes it easier to discipline them."

A friend of mine told me of how her elementary school years were scarred by mob mentality. Oddly enough she became a teacher and lived to tell about it. She said she felt that she was always in trouble for fidgeting and her attention deficit hyperac-tivity, but instead of compassion, she was dealt anger.

In relaying her story, she told me about good old Mrs. May-field, who affected her for the rest of her life. "Mrs. Mayfield's cure for my restlessness? She had one strategy—the 'We can all thank Nancy' strategy. She punished *everybody* everytime I was out of line. 'We're not having recess today, and do you know who we can all thank? We can all thank Nancy!' At least twice a week for all of third grade, she would do this to me. 'Yes, that's right, we can all thank Nancy. Because Nancy was not paying attention...was out of her seat... was not following directions...Yes, you can all thank Nancy for not having recess today, perhaps you can thank Nancy next time we have a recess, if...of course we ever have another recess...perhaps we'll wait and see if Nancy will ever follow directions well enough so that we can!'"

My friend said that she would never forget how Mrs. Mayfield made her feel. Daily she makes a conscious effort never to use these "isolating" techniques. We all know what happens to children who are isolated from others. It hurts, and there are a lot of tears as their classmates walk by and say, "Thanks a lot Nancy...Way to go Nancy! We hate you Nancy...It's your fault Nancy!"

As was the case with my friend, she didn't realize how mean Mrs. Mayfield was until she grew up and could understand the teacher's passive-aggressive behavior. I'm sure if there's a hell for Mrs. Mayfield, she's probably there, tied to the jungle gym and surrounded by hundreds of hyperactive children.

Peaceful people continually influence their world, and never give up on it. They never give up on children, and they always seem to have a sense of hope for a child's future. They don't destroy a child's connection to others. No matter how much a child rubs them the wrong way, they are always trying to make a stronger bond, a kinship with him.

There are times for all of us when we need others for support. When we have problems, we may discuss them with other professionals, or talk to friends, or family. Most of the time we are trying to get an objective viewpoint that may either help us or clarify the direction we need to pursue. We have also recognized when people become neurotic about their own issues and, in an odd way they want to gang up on someone. Somehow it makes their weak ego feel stronger (if only momentarily).

We all have a co-worker who is at odds with someone and goes out of his way to get everyone on his side. Rather than trying to go about solving the problem, he wants to let everyone else know they should also be mad, angry, or at odds with the person he can't get along with. He will try to get the rumor mill going (as a result of his own discomfort). He believes that "if everyone feels the way I do toward this person, then I'm okay!"

When people set off on these missions to "get everyone on their side," two things remain the same; first, it doesn't help the person they are in conflict with, and secondly, in the long run—it doesn't solve their own problems. The neurotic remain neurotic.

It is important to remember that mob mentality can only destroy others' lives. It's no wonder that children end up becoming hostile toward others when we separate them with these tactics. Think about the last time you knew an adult who lost relationships or respect, because of someone's malicious need to create an alignment.

Three out of four instances of violence in schools begin with children saying they need to "get even" with someone. If they believe that someone is on their side, they may not have the need to "get even." If a child perceives fairness in his communication with adults, he won't have as strong a need to take justice into his own hands, and it will pave the way to an open door for communication.

When we condemn a child with isolation tactics we are no better than other "hateful" people who have tried to change others through hurting them. Prejudice, bigotry, oppression, and terrorism can only destroy, not build humanity. It doesn't take a lot to be an activist for children (or for ethical humane behavior), sometimes it just takes day-to-day kindness.

> **We cannot change anything until we accept it. Condemnation does not liberate, it oppresses.**
>
> **Carl Jung**

Bully Kids Become Bully Adults

> **Never be bullied into silence. Never allow yourself to be made a victim. Accept no one's definition of your life. Define yourself.**
>
> **Harvey Feinstein**

"Oh, kids will be kids!" This is a statement that we often hear about the playground bully. Or, we may hear, "Children just need to learn to toughen up and stand up to that bully."

The problem with both of the statements is that we are accepting violence and intolerance. Neither address a solution. If a co-worker or a boss is abusive, we take appropriate measures. We don't say, "Oh, those cute bosses. Bosses will be bosses!" When we are confronted with an abusive person, we don't just say, "Oh just punch that co-worker right between the eyes; that will solve the problem!"

The bullies in our culture often push us into one of two ineffective responses. One is of aggression; the other is of silence. Effective schools and families know that the only way to move toward change is to stop the bullying in its tracks. This is done by addressing *all* behaviors that seek to take advantage of others, harm others, oppress others, or deny others their right to grow.

Unfortunately, many parents are simply relieved if their child is not a victim. The child learns from their parents to look the other way. When a group of sixth graders was asked about intervening in bullying acts, the most often cited response was, "I would like to stop it, but I'm afraid that if I try, they will come after me." We have to empower children to solve their own problems, and if a major crime occurs then we have to call in a legal system that will protect them. How would we act if we called the police and they responded, "Hey pal, just learn to toughen up. So what if your neighbor is shooting at you!"

Effective schools bring issues of character into all aspects of their education. In doing so, they are changing social norms in the children and adults. This sense of empowerment allows them to utilize human kinship to solve human problems.

Several things these schools are doing make a difference. First, they are asking all those who were innocent bystanders to enhance their connections to the children. All teachers, cafeteria workers, bus drivers, hall monitors, secretaries, and custodians are asked to greet children, learn their names, and get to know them. It only makes sense—when you feel connected to someone, you feel indebted to them. When you feel indebted to someone, you are unlikely to hurt him.

Secondly, effective schools are integrating issues of character into their reading lists, classes, lessons, and recess programs. Lastly, and most importantly, they are asking the children to help. They are connecting older children to younger children. They are starting discussions with fifth and sixth graders about how they felt when they were younger, and if they felt hurt by others and left out.

These schools are discovering that when they asked the bullies to help, often there was an unprecedented transformation in their behavior. It happens for the same reason that some of our best inner city youth counselors are former gang members. It's taking the child with no purpose in their connections and giving them meaning in their lives. It would be naïve to think that it works for all bullies, but astonishingly enough, some of them have taken enormous pride in their training to be peer counselors or peer mediators.

We cannot change all behaviors in all children, but those schools integrating character education are making dramatic reductions in fights and suspensions. Creating a climate of respect and having vigilance for addressing every instance, changes schools dramatically. As an unexpected bonus, administrators are also changing some of the grumpy behavior of their own employees.

Our schools will always have problems, some are overloaded with dysfunctional students who often come from dysfunctional families, and some are overloaded with dysfunctional employees as well, but the bottom line is this—a system that diligently creates its boundaries, behaviors, and norms will change its citizens. A system that focuses on building behaviors—rather than punishing for the lack of them—will bring about the greatest changes in its members.

Bullies have the same need as others to feel worthwhile. The flaw in their thinking is that they are insecure in their ability to work with others; they lack the skill of creating healthy connections. Bullies can be any age; the characteristics of their personalities are all the same. They've learned to get their needs met only through dominating others. Bully adults are the same as bully children: they can't let their guard down, they feel uneasy if they are vulnerable, and they see domination (as opposed to cooperation) as a means to get the job done. Their judgment of the inferiority of others becomes a mainstay in their philosophy of life.

> **The nobler a person, the harder it is to suspect inferiority in others.**
>
> **Marcus Tullius Cicero**

Quite often bullies did not learn how to handle a situation when they were dominated. They formed an illogical connection—*controlling others is the best way to have one's needs met.* The research shows us that the number one predictor for violence in teenagers is if they came from homes that verbally or physically abused them. Unfortunately, as adults they don't understand the loneliness that may ensue as a result of continuing this way of thinking and acting. What is at stake is a lifelong inability to accept and connect to others.

At the core of intolerance is "price tagging." Bullies learn at an early age that they need to price-tag people in order to have self-worth; they like to get even instead of collaborate, because they feel they've lost power when they are on everyone else's level. The best way to teach acceptance to others is to give the child an environment where price-tagging doesn't take place. We use language to make our lives more effective, but sometimes we abuse language to create a false sense of superiority. A term such as "depression" or "bulimia" or "anxiety" may help us to find the best treatment for a person who is suffering from a set of symptoms. On the other hand, if we create images in our minds for African-American, Jew, feminist, athlete, Asian, elderly, we become captive to the term. We've given up our ability to go beyond the term and ask—is she kind? Does he love his children? Is she thoughtful? Is he compassionate toward others?

When we let go of our price tags, we let go of our biases.

One-Minute Reflection: Isolation

There's probably no feeling of sadness quite like that we experience when we feel cut off and isolated from others. When we are bullied into isolation and silence, we begin to second guess our self-worth. It's important that we reflect on how isolating affects our lives, and if we are in fact isolating others.

___Did I "price tag" anyone for our differences today?

___What did I do if overheard "price tagging" today?

___How do I react to bullies? Do I let them become the judge of my character?

___How much power did I relinquish in my life to others?

___Did I let the bullying in life trickle down? If I was bullied, then did I take out my frustrations on others?

___Was I a passive observer to another's meanness today?

Invitations for Camaraderie

This country will not be a good place for any of us to live unless we make it a good place for all of us to live.

Theodore Roosevelt

Some time ago I read in the paper that a teacher had taken a complaint to his union. The complaint was from a high school where the teachers were asked to stand outside their classrooms, in the hall, between every class to cut down on school violence and bullying. The teacher complained because it wasn't part of the contract.

That reminded me of my student teaching assignment several decades ago. I was assigned to a high school teacher who the students affectionately called Mr. Q. He was a big man in his late fifties with the energy of a child and the heart of a saint. When I started, he told me to show up an hour early to school everyday. For that semester, I faithfully did that everyday. During that time he would visit the cooks, the custodians, the secretaries, and other service people in the building. He did this every single day without fail. He told me, "These are the most important people in your building—try to live without food, a warm room, and someone to help you when the ditto machine is broke—believe me you won't get far."

Mr. Q also had these monstrous hands that would envelope your hand when he shook it. And this man shook hands—sometimes hundreds of times each day. And this is what I remember the most—my first day of school when the bell rang he turned to me and asked, "Do you want to get to know the kids? Follow me." Every single day of my student teaching I followed behind this man as he walked from one end of the building to the other. He must have known more than 500 kids by their first names. His thunderous barreling voice would nearly shake the halls, "Good Morning! Good Morning! How are you doing today? Good Morning!" Soon I found myself doing the same thing, and it was the best teaching experience I have ever.

Since that time I've read numerous professional teaching journals that talk about "Connecting with kids, creating the peaceable school, and developing character." In all of those articles they talk about "getting to know kids, reaching out to kids, and empathizing with kids." Heck, Mr. Q knew this before it ever made it to a research journal.

I taught Health Education that semester, and I probably can't remember one or two things that I taught, but I do remember what I learned. In this day and age of incivility and buzzwords like "connecting with kids," I saw someone who actually did it. There was also something that happened on the last day of school that I will never forget. Numerous students dropped by and thanked him, and many of the high school seniors also tearfully hugged him. There was also one young woman who quietly dropped a card on his desk, thanked him, and walked out. Mr. Q read the card then handed it to me and said, "This is why I teach."

In the card the young woman wrote, "Dear Mr. Q, I'm now graduating and I only have one regret and that's that I never got to be in one of your classes. I've got to tell you, however, that the best part of my day—every day, was your smile. Thank you. Annette."

From that day forward, I had one wish, and that was one day to be, "that person" in some student's life. It's the most important lesson I ever learned in education. To those teachers who are complaining to their union, I feel sad for what they are missing out on. To Mr. Q, wherever you are, thanks.

The best that any of us could hope for would be to be that special person in someone's life. We need to ask ourselves, how will my family, students, co-workers, neighbors, and friends think back and remember me? Will they remember "your smile" as the best part of their day?

> **Why, even when I was teaching, there were plenty of times when my students came up with better ideas than I had. And why shouldn't they? Just because I was the teacher, it didn't mean I knew everything.**
>
> **Sadie Delaney**
> ***The Delaney Sisters—Book of Everyday Wisdom***

In the push for peaceful schools, it is widely recognized that students who are involved in after-school programs have lifelong lowered incidences of drug and alcohol abuse, and incidences of serious violence. The reason for this is children who connect in various social settings have the opportunity to develop greater social skills. In these arenas they have more opportunities to learn the values of cooperation, teamwork, trust, and leadership. They also have greater opportunities to develop communication skills, to give and accept feedback. It doesn't matter whether the child is involved in the debate club, the orchestra, the science club, or the track team. The results are all the same. Children are given greater opportunities to develop relationships with mentors, coaches, and other strong adult key figures in their lives. Most of all, however, they are able to connect with something and work toward a goal that is bigger than themselves. Children join a gang or a cult for the same reasons that they join the basketball team—being a part of *anything* is more important than being a part of nothing at all.

One of the most common characteristics of children who may have a proneness to violence is the feeling of social isolation. When children are connected, they develop a greater sense of self-worth. Most of us can even reflect on the power of connections in our own lives. Corporate executives know that if their employees feel connected, their self-worth and productivity increase. In all of our lives we can reflect on times when being a part of something was great.

Being a part of *anything* may be one of the most powerful experiences in our lives. We should never underestimate how an invitation for kinship and camaraderie may be a life-changing event. The best jobs we've ever had, and the best memories we've experienced have to do with our kinship to others. We never seem to miss cars, houses, and other possessions that come and go, as much as we miss people. That feeling of connection made us feel whole.

I still think about the parents who agonized over their disconnected and bullied children. Their children suffered the fate of being placed on the "outside" by their peers. When our needs are not being met in life, we become most vulnerable to compromising our ethical judgment and our sense of good. We create our own beasts that tear down others' lives. In this case, their children were at the mercy of other children's insecurities. Children will do anything to avoid being "on the outside." Our job is to destroy and eliminate the concept of the "outside."

We cannot make a rule for or legislate kinship. It has to grow from education about a connected and united humanity where social justice is more than just a catch phrase, until it becomes the norm on our playgrounds, schools, neighborhoods, and workplaces. Kind adults produce kind children. Kind people make it a better world for all of us to live in. Rising above the insanity and teaching our children to jump past the obstacles of intolerance will send freedom into the next generation. Extending opportunities for kinship will result in our children one day extending it themselves.

One-Minute Reflection: Camaraderie

Compassion and love are not static entities.

1. We either grow in love each day of our lives, or we lose love each day of our lives.

2. How many invitations for camaraderie and kinship did you extend today?

3. Even if you were afraid, did you extend yourself?

4. If you were too afraid to extend yourself, what choice stood in your way?

5. If you were too proud to extend yourself, what choice stood in your way?

My favorite character in all of sports history was Jackie Robinson. Jackie was asked to be patient during his early years as the first African-American major league baseball player. During that time he endured taunts and racial slurs that would cause most of us to give up on life. Toward the end of his life, he did not show patience. He showed impatience, but it was the kind of impatience that deserved the highest respect. Jackie pushed harder for civil rights in his years after baseball than he did during his baseball career. He said, "I don't want to leave this world with a *promise* that one day my child will have equality. I want you to give me equality today, then I will *know* that my child will have it tomorrow."

Perhaps the best way to teach kinship today is to give it today.

Living our Lessons
The Only Way to Teach Character is to Live Character

> **Loving can cost a lot, but not loving costs more.**
>
> **Merle Shain**

Love's Opposite

Leo Buscaglia was the author of numerous books on love, caring, and human compassion. He once said, "The opposite of love is not hate, it is apathy." He believed that we lose love when we give up on it. We lose love when we give up on others.

How many times have we heard someone say, "There's nothing I can do about that kid!" Our biggest enemy in the development of human character is not hate, aggression, or anger—**our biggest enemy is apathy.**

When we give up on our profession, a child, or the world, we have given up all of the power we have. Each person who works with a child occupies a piece of the pie; we each influence the outcome of that child's future. For some it may be a large slice of the pie, and others—very small. In any case, we all add something to others' lives in all we do.

This applies to the world as well, every time we rage at, scream at, or demean another, we've made the world a lesser place. We have to avoid the idea that, because we are adults, we have a license to violate others with our loss of control. We need to model our behavior.

198

In modeling the behavior we want in children, we take responsibility, and begin to shape the entire environment. If we want a peaceful world, we have to start by making our piece the most warm, special, productive, caring, and compassionate piece of all. Children will always remember the piece of their lives that you occupy. In fact, your piece of the pie may be the very one that sweetens the entire pie. Your piece may be the very one that restores the child's faith in humanity. We should never lose our faith in our ability to make a difference; it may be the most valuable thing we ever possess.

Chase After Truth

> **Chase after truth like all hell, and you will free yourself; even though you'll never touch its coattails.**
>
> **Clarence Darrow**

We need to set up our lives so that we never stop chasing the truth. Peaceful, tolerant people are always seeking wisdom. They have a sense of reverence for those who have created lives that have a wealth of goodness, compassion, and understanding.

Loving and compassionate people carefully choose their heroes and their crusades. Blamers worship other blamers and are capable of creating nothing more than a crusade of anger. The future of our children's character is bound by the decisions that the adults are making in their lives.

> ## It is never too late to be what you might have been.
>
> ### George Eliot

Life is like school. Not every day is an "A" day. All of us will have B, C, D, and—sadly enough—F days as well. Like school though, we need to stay focused on learning continually, rather than on scoring 100 on every test. If we are expecting perfect grades, we are on a collision course with disaster.

Some days we will be less than civil, less than patient, and we will be less than perfect. How will we make it right? Blame the school? Or, stay after school and get it right? Can we admit our faults? Let our guard down? Apologize? Forgive? Try again?

A computer can run a program perfectly. We will never run our lives perfectly. We need to hope for progress and a continual learning process. Our energy, motivation, enthusiasm, and hope will all ebb and flow. Give yourself a break when it happens. Forget about perfect, be today's best and keep in mind what's at stake. What's at stake is our future and the future of our children. We don't have to be perfect, but we may have to do things differently. As Albert Einstein once said, "The problems that exist in the world today cannot be solved by the level of thinking that created them." It's new thinking that creates new results.

> **No act of kindness, no matter how small,
> is ever wasted**
>
> **Aesop**

Kindness and character are not "once and for all" things. They grow through a continuous effort and an investment. What we do today will feed tomorrow's aggression. What we do today will also create tomorrow's kindness and character.

Index

A

Aesop, 201

agent of change, 19, 44

aggression, 4, 6, 7, 13, 25, 32, 42, 63, 64, 68, 69, 100, 143, 152, 172, 174, 178, 188, 198, 201

anger, 13, 31, 47, 63, 65, 68, 69, 74, 75, 79-81, 100, 107, 109, 120, 123, 146, 151, 152, 161, 181, 184, 198, 199

angry, 4, 39, 44, 79, 80, 106, 107, 119, 151, 152, 155, 160, 163, 186, 201

Anthony, Robert, 116

anti-social, 22

B

Barrymore, Ethel, 75

Berra, Yogi, 9

blame, 20, 29, 91, 94, 121, 136, 148, 153, 154, 180, 181, 184, 195, 200

Brady Bunch, 21

Browne, H. Jackson, 49, 173

bullied, bullies, bully, 1-3, 9, 13, 58, 62, 78, 172, 173, 181, 188-192, 196

Burke, Edmund, 23

C

camaraderie, 192, 196, 197

Carter, Jimmy, 126, 201

character, 5, 8, 11, 17, 19, 27, 28, 79, 133, 166, 183, 189, 192, 193, 198, 199, 201

character education, 1, 10, 15, 143, 190

D

203

E

F

G

guilt, 58, 66, 67, 69, 70, 121, 122, 138

H

Holmes, Oliver Wendell, 1
Hooks, Benjamin, 126
hope, 10, 53, 125, 126, 147, 167, 171, 174, 185, 194, 200,
hostility, 10, 44, 71, 77, 108, 113, 119, 172, 175, 180, 182
Howard, Dale, 10, 117, 118
Hungarian proverb, 66

I

impulse control, 16, 27, 111
incivility, incivilities, 18, 19, 21, 23, 24, 32, 44, 49, 68, 181, 193,
incompetence, 157, 159-161
isolation, 173, 183, 186, 192, 195

J

Joubert, Joseph, 60
Jeffy, 73, 74
Jung, Carl, 175, 180, 187

K

Keller, Helen, 175
kindness, 7, 8, 16, 27, 33, 42-44, 54, 60, 69, 70, 103, 107, 108, 119, 120, 166, 174, 187, 201
King, Martin Luther, 9, 82, 126, 148, 176, 183,
kinship, 13, 168, 171-173, 185, 189, 196, 197

L

label, labeling, 31, 33, 38, 39, 40, 82

lashing, 58, 63, 68, 71, 107, 108, 115, 134, 151, 159

laugh, laughing, laughter, 4, 36, 37, 58, 71, 72, 74-76, 78, 86, 97, 112, 117, 122,

life-skills, 5, 7, 10, 134, 147

Lincoln, Abraham, 144

listening, 3, 78, 94, 133, 159, 174

Lombardi, Vince, 100

M, N

Magic wand, 8

Mandela, Nelson, 126

Maslow, Abraham, 44,

mean, meanness, 4349, 61, 68, 77, 107, 139-142, 148, 150, 151, 159, 169, 170, 184, 185, 192

misery, miserable, 31, 38, 44, 45, 60-63, 65, 70-72, 77, 78, 80, 81, 87-89, 90, 91, 94, 97, 106, 108, 112, 113, 116, 122, 146, 151, 154, 160, 162, 166, 175, 181,

Mortman, Doris, 37

Mother Theresa, 87, 126, 129

O

obsess, obsessing, obsession, 7, 60, 61, 66, 79, 81, 84, 97, 113, 138, 154, 158

obstacles, 12, 20, 88, 89, 93, 94, 120, 174, 176, 196

oppress, oppressive, oppression, 9, 12, 126, 127, 131, 142, 143, 171-173, 177, 178, 187, 188

optimism, optimistic, 12, 44, 91, 116-120

P

Q

R

S

T

U, V

W, X, Y, Z

Dr. Stephen Birchak

     Dr. Stephen Birchak has worked in higher education for more than 25 years. He is a widely known authority and speaker in the field of aggression and violence, and the co-author of the *Champions of Dignity*—a series of stories about non-violent superheroes for elementary school children. Educated at Adams State College, Colorado (M.A.), and the University of Northern Colorado (B.A.. and Ed.D.), Dr. Birchak is currently a Professor of Counseling Psychology at The College of Saint Rose in Albany, New York. Thousands of counselors, teachers, administrators, psychologists, and parents have attended his violence prevention and character education workshops. His stories, examples, and educational psychology principles have been the cornerstone of his speaking engagements. Dr. Birchak emphasizes a solution-focused philosophy that asks parents, schools, and communities to work together to create peaceful communities. His efforts toward influencing nonviolence in children have become a poignant and timely topic not only for the present but also for our future.

Some Comments

"This is a treasure of a book! Dr. Birchak's lessons make it the perfect book for parents, school leaders, counselors, and teachers."

> Dr. Perry Berkowitz, Ed.D., President, PLB Consulting, Retired Superintendent, Professor, Vestal, New York

"As a psychologist, educator, and parent, I couldn't agree more with the exceptional wisdom in this book. Dr. Birchak has a warm and engaging writing style that invites the reader in and encourages self-reflection. This book would be a terrific gift. A 'must read' on every parent, teacher, and caregivers reading list!"

> Dr. Donna Burns Ph.D., Educational Psychology Professor, The College of Saint Rose, Albany, New York

"'How to Build a Child's Character' has the ability to be humane and speak to the matter in such a way that will inspire anyone who works with children. In my 30 years as an educational administrator, I have had the opportunity to train with and be inspired by some of the best in the business. I have never known anyone do a better job than Dr. Birchak. He is simply one of the best."

> Sean Casey M.S.—School Principal, Educational Administrator, Penobscot, Maine

"A most valuable resource for parents, teachers, and adults. This book provides essential principles and strategies for fostering caring and civility in our daily lives. Definitely a must read!!!"

Dr. Nicole Chase Ph.D., Counseling Professor, St. Lawrence University

"This book is a call to arms (the embracing kind) for all of us who work with children! Dr. Birchak has given educators and parents a great gift with this thought-provoking and honest work. He eloquently demonstrates the value of teaching compassion to children by being compassionate ourselves."

Pamela Birnbach M.S., Director of Guidance Services, Academy of the Holy Names High School, Albany, New York